African Identity in Asia

African
Identity
in Asia

Cultural Effects
of Forced Migration

Shihan de Silva Jayasuriya

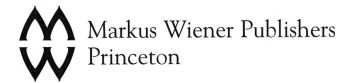 Markus Wiener Publishers
Princeton

For information, write to
Markus Wiener Publishers
231 Nassau Street, Princeton, NJ 08542
www.markuswiener.com

Library of Congress Cataloging-in-Publication Data
Jayasuriya, Shihan de S.
    African identity in Asia : cultural effects of forced migration /
Shihan de Silva Jayasuriya.
        p. cm.
    Includes bibliographical references and index.
    ISBN 978-1-55876-471-2 (hardcover : alk. paper)
    ISBN 978-1-55876-472-9 (paperback : alk. paper)
    1. Africans—Asia. 2. Forced migration—Africa. 3.
Asia—Emigration and immigration. I. Title.
    DS28.A35J39 2008
    305.896'05—dc22
                                                    2008008592

Markus Wiener Publishers books are printed in the United States of
America on acid-free paper and meet the guidelines for permanence
and durability of the Committee on Production Guidelines for Book
Longevity of the Council on Library Resources.

For my parents
Dr. Anthony Roland Fairlye de Silva
and
Mrs. Pearl de Silva
who pointed the way

Contents

Illustrations

Foreword

There are a handful of studies on Africans in Asia which have not reached a wide readership. They have mainly concentrated on individual populations within national boundaries in Asia. More than ever, it is necessary to attempt some wider survey of the African presence throughout Asia.

Since slavery is part of world history, it is important to present a comprehensive description of events and not simply a one-sided story that is limited only to the Atlantic world. The searing focus given to transatlantic slavery this year has aroused interest in the general population about this part of our history. This is a time when there is a keen interest in other migrations. The eastward movement of Africans is, of course, an old phenomenon which goes back almost two millennia. The myriad of ethnonyms and varied sociopolitical circumstances complicate the study of Afro-Asians. This book enlightens us on the eastward migration of Africans.

Africa's past is important in understanding contemporary African affairs. The African diaspora is a complicated one. In addition to the Atlantic world, the trajectory of slavery cut into the Islamic world and the Indian Ocean. Although many have assimilated into their host communities, they are still recognizable and identifiable in Asia today. Africans who were outsiders have now become insiders in Asia.

This book uncovers a very important topic and goes beyond historical accounts and archival sources. By not limiting herself to a single community or country and through the impetus gained by researching the Africans in Sri Lanka, Shihan de Silva Jayasuriya deals with the presence of Africans in Asia, which has been overlooked for too long. No doubt, this book will be a catalyst for other scholarly works to follow in the coming years. The wider significance of her work may well be in attracting others to this complex and fascinating field.

RICHARD PANKHURST
Professor of Ethiopian Studies
Addis Ababa University
Ethiopia

Preface

The movement of African peoples to Asia drew my attention when I came across the largest community of Afro-Sri Lankans in the northwestern village of Sirambiyadiya, Sri Lanka. Having researched their mother-tongue, I was able to surprise the elders of the community by conversing with them in the Indo-Portuguese of Ceylon. Struck by their varied physiognomy, music, and dance, I began to search for their roots. This led me to Professor Richard Pankhurst, the Ethiopianist, who was equally enthusiastic when I showed him a few of my recordings of this community. Our collaboration resulted in a co-edited book, *The African Diaspora in the Indian Ocean*, which Africa World Press, in Trenton, New Jersey, published in 2003. It includes a collection of articles by Edward Alpers (University of California, U.S.), Eduardo Medeiros (University of Evora, Portugal), Malyn Newitt (King's College London, University of London, U.K.), Helen Hintjens (University of Swansea, Wales), Jean Houbert (University of Aberdeen, Scotland), Helene Basu (Free University, Germany), Richard Pankhurst (Addis Ababa University, Ethiopia) and Shihan de Silva Jayasuriya (University of London).

Soon after I began to search for other Afro-Asian communities. In this book, by making comparisons and not limiting my study to a single Asian country, I aim to map the migration of Africans to Asia and their contributions to their host societies. While slavery and the slave trade have underpinned African migration, they tend to obscure the African contributions, most notably in military activities and music. Africans in Asia should not be viewed solely as descendants of slaves; they should be recognized as cultural brokers between continents. Having lived in Africa and Asia, I can appreciate the links between the two peoples.

While many Africans have assimilated into their host societies and are unidentifiable within communities, a few of them, who are hidden away in forests and villages, still maintain a distinct identity. There are several complex issues relating to the identity of these communities. The scholar faces many challenges, often working with limited archival sources, oral histories, folklore, and oral traditions.

I hope that the interest shown in transatlantic migrants has now aroused sufficient curiosity in scholars, policymakers, welfare agencies, and international organizations such as the United Nations to prompt them to study other African migrations across the Indian Ocean and beyond.

Acknowledgements

I am grateful to my parents, Dr. Fairlye de Silva and Mrs. Pearl de Silva, who exposed me to urban and rural Sri Lankan life. They also taught me to play the piano well enough to earn a Diploma from the Trinity College of Music (London) and encouraged me to perform the Sri Lankan Kandyan dance, influencing my sensitivity to artistic expressions.

I wish to thank the Afro-Sri Lankans in Puttalama who inspired me with their spontaneous performances of traditional music and dance. Thanks are also due to the Calouste Gulbenkian Foundation and the Fundação Oriente for funding my fieldwork in Puttalama, Sri Lanka.

I should like to thank my husband, Dr. Hemal Jayasuriya, for the two poems that appear in this book and for his constructive comments on the text. Last but not least, I appreciate the patience of my son, Johan Heshan, during the many hours I spent working on this book.

Glossary

Abed	a black slave
Baila	a genre of popular music, song, and dance in Sri Lanka
Bori	a spirit possession cult (Hausa word)
Caliph	title for successor among Muslims
Caliphate	a Muslim state that is headed by a Caliph
Chaush	Afro-Hyderabadis
Dargah	a shrine
Dhows	a traditional sailing vessel
Fakir	a Sufi mendicant
Ghulam	male black slaves
Habshi	an ethnonym for Africans in Asia
Hajj	the pilgrimage made by Muslims to the holy sites
Jāti	an Indian caste
Kaffir/Coffree	an ethnonym for Africans in Asia
Kaffrinha	a genre of music, song, and dance in Sri Lanka
Kanis	black female slaves
Khaneshad	children of slaves
Mamluk	a white slave
Mu'adhdhin	one who calls the Muslims to prayer
Murgu	the system in which slaves were allowed to work on their own
Qawal	devotional songs
Sidi	an ethnonym for Afro-Indians
Tanburah	lyre
Zar	a spirit possession cult

CHAPTER 1

Eastbound Africans

African migration is intertwined with a number of issues: slavery, slave trading, integration, social mobility, assimilation, marriage, miscegenation, religious conversion, colonization, decolonization, self-expression, ethnic and cultural identities. The history of displaced communities is central to these wide-ranging issues, which require models of slavery other than the transatlantic one. Historically, slavery—even in contemporary terms—has never been a simple question of East and West. In addition, western historical studies usually lack the lived-in experience of contemporary Asian societies, omitting, for instance, the sounds of Africa in remote villages in Sri Lanka and the forests of India. Questions related to how, why and when Africans settled in Asia arise as well. This book draws attention to the presence of sub-Saharan Africans and their descendants in Asia (Chapter 2).

Slavery and slave trading have often been researched by historians who tend to question the existence of social systems. Generally, historians think that social systems fail to provide the primary explanations for social reality. However, world-systems analysts, who stress that all social systems are simultaneously systemic and historical—that is, they evolve continuously and are never static from one time period to the next—have adopted an approach that is better suited for analyzing slavery and the slave trading which have occurred over several millennia. This hermeneutical approach allows the researcher to empathize with and interpret a particular social situation, as opposed to using a set of objective modes of knowlege such as statistical analysis. For every kind of social time, there is a particular kind of social space. When analyzing sit-

1

uations in social systems, one should not measure time and space separately, as they are always linked.

In the Iberian Peninsula and most of the Mediterranean world, slavery was an institution. Aristotle defined a slave as "a living tool, a tool which can move and talk with some amount of intelligence" (Coupland 1933:1–2). Roman and canon law as well as the Bible and the Aristotelian philosophy allowed slavery to be a part of the universal social order (Saunders 1982:35). By the end of the Middle Ages, Roman and canon law decreed that prisoners of war and criminals could become slaves, children of slaves were also slaves, and slaves could be bought and sold like chattels. In chattel slavery, one human being had power to sell and transfer ownership, thus controlling the slave's home life, daily activities, and children. In Christianity, a chattel slave had no rights since they had been transferred to the owner. Miers (2004:4) points out that unlike those in the West, slaves in the Islamic world were protected by Islamic laws.

In the Atlantic world, the slave was a chattel who labored in plantations and mines. In the Indian Ocean world, however, slaves performed a variety of tasks as, for example, sailors, soldiers, musicians, water carriers, road builders, seamstresses, concubines, palace guards, body guards, harem guards, and pearl fishers. Some slaves were financially better off than free people because they performed very specialized tasks. Campbell (2004:xii) argues that slaves in the Indian Ocean world enjoyed an array of traditional and prescribed rights and protection which was uncommon in the Atlantic world.

What part did the slave trade play in displacing Africans across continents? Is the emphasis placed upon it justified? Defining and distinguishing slavery from other forms of bondage have challenged scholars. The limitations of the use of the Atlantic model in the study of Indian Oceanic migration have been acknowledged for some time. In this book, migration is defined as the movement of people. In Asia, systems of servitude and bondage were influenced by eastern philosophies and practices unknown to the Atlantic world. This affected the process of assimilation and social mobility of migrants. While economic advancement enables social mobility in America, intermarriage is a driving force behind assimilation in the East (see Chapter 6).

In addition, a distinction needs to be made between slavery and the slave trade. Slavery has been an important part of the social and economic life of all countries since antiquity. According to historical records, slavery dates back to 2900 BCE. Egyptian paintings depicted Nubian captives being enslaved by the Egyptians in a boat on the Nile River. The slave trade represents a commodification of human beings, indistinguishable from other economic goods such as pepper and cinnamon.

Oral histories play an important role in the construction of African history, as the past is otherwise revealed only through archaeological research and occasional accounts from non-African observers. Most historians have failed to recognize the African cultural expressions and presence in contemporary Asian societies. The emphasis placed on slavery dangerously obscures other aspects of culture including its maintenance and transformations.

Historical Background

Migration usually never happens *en bloc*. The eastward migration from Africa has been largely forced, though trading contacts existed between the two continents (de Silva Jayasuriya 2004a). Occurring over several centuries, migration reflects the demand from various buyers—Arabs, Indians, Portuguese, Dutch, French, and British.

Migration is often twofold, voluntary and involuntary. Commercial contacts between Africa and Asia date back several millennia. Archaeological findings also confirm ancient links between the two continents. Between the third century BC and the second century, Indian figurines were known to have been imported to the Aksumite kingdom (Contenson 1965:45–47). Over a hundred Kushana gold coins from around 230 AD were discovered in Dabra Damo which is located in northern Ethiopia (Matthews and Mordini 1959). Aksum (in today's Ethiopia) flourished from the first to the seventh centuries, and the fact that Aksum coins from the fourth century were found in Mangalore, India, indicates commercial contacts between India and Ethiopia. For example, seventeen gold coins, dated around 320, were discovered from the reign of the Aksumite king Ousanas; six from around 333, during the reign of Esana, the first Christian King of Aksum, have been found (Baptiste, McLeod, and Robbins 2006:18).

The anonymous Egyptian Greek author of *Periplus of the Erythraean Sea*, a text that dates back to the first century, mentions commercial contacts between southwestern Arabia and the East African littoral (Huntingford 1980). According to Basu (1993:291), the African presence in the Indian subcontinent dates back to the first century. In the year 77, according to Pliny's accounts, the town of Barygasa (today's Bharuch [Broach] in Gujarat) was considerd an "Ethiopian" town (Wink 1990).

Abyssinians traded in Mātota (near Mannar in the northwestern province of Sri Lanka) during the fifth century (Gibb 1929). Cosmas Indicopleustes, a sixth century Egyptian traveler, states that Ethiopians from Adulis traded in Taprobane (a Hellenization of the Sinhala word *Tambapanni*), which is called Sri Lanka today (McCrindle 1897). from the Horn—mercenaries, sailors, and traders—migrated voluntarily to Asia (Alpers 2003).

The slave trade sapped Africa of its human resources through various routes across the Sahara desert, the Red Sea, and the Indian and Atlantic Ocean ports of Africa. From the ninth to the nineteenth centuries, Islamic societies benefited from African slavery. This overlapped with more than four hundred years of slave trade that began at the end of the fifteenth century.

In the sixteenth century, people from Russia, Ukraine, and the Balkan states were enslaved in the Ottoman Empire (Lovejoy 2004a:27). Until at least the beginning of the nineteenth century, both black Muslim and white Christian slaves could be found in the Ottoman and Maghreb areas. The Turks preferred African slaves while the Greeks had a preference for Bulgar slaves (Inalcik and Quartaert 1994:729). The caravan trade from the south of the Arabian Peninsula had trade links with Africa and the East. From the eighteenth century onwards, Ethiopians also came to India with the spread of Islam.

The sixteenth-century Portuguese traveler, Tomé Pires (1944:268),

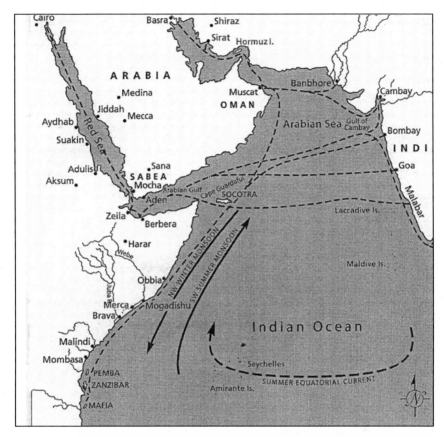

The Indian Ocean, the Red Sea, and the Sabaean Lane
(Source: Robert Collins, *African & Asian* Studies, 2006)

mentioned that Abyssinians and Africans from Kilwa and Malindi were trading in Malacca, implying that the long established trading links between Africa and Asia already existed when the Europeans started to sail the Indian Ocean.

The trade in black slaves cannot be attributed to Europeans alone. Prior to European expansion overseas, the Africans living in lands between the Niger and Dar-Fur were bought and sold in East African markets, which were governed by Islamic principles forbidding that a fellow Muslim be enslaved. Neither slavery nor the slave trade, however, was created by Islam (Braudel 1993:130). By the Middle Ages, two Arabic words referred to slaves based on color—a black slave was usually called *abed* while a white slave was called *mamluk* (Segal 2001:49).

Egyptian art depicts African slaves among pharaohs. The Hellenistic and Roman worlds also had African slaves. Even in pre-Islamic times, Arabs owned East African slaves. As the crossroads of the caravan routes to Arabia, Mecca developed a major slave market. The Ka'ba, a religious shrine in Mecca, attracted devotees who worshiped tribal deities and came on annual pilgrimages to pay their respects.

After conquering the Middle East, Persia, and North Africa by the tenth century, Arabs absorbed the historic institution of slavery, which was then transformed to suit Islamic laws and practices. Previously established commercial networks enabled Muslim traders to indulge in enslaving Africans. Lombard (1971) points out that only Muslims or *dhimmī*—subjects of the Head of the Islamic state, such as Jews, Christians, Sabeans (a Mandean Judeo-Christian sect)—or Zoroastrians were permitted within the frontiers. None of them could be reduced to slavery; however, there were a few exceptions such as the Copts of the Delta, who revolted and were therefore led away to slavery. The difficulty of enslaving those within the frontiers of Islam provided the impetus for obtaining slaves from outside. Once captives converted to Islam, they were liberated from slavery—and this resulted in a greater demand for Africans. Converted slaves became *mawālī* (clients) of the Prophet and other prominent Muslims. As long as an African was not a Muslim, he or she could be enslaved and transported across the Sahara desert, Red Sea, and Indian Ocean. Unlike those who converted to Christianity, Islamic converts were emancipated. Outside the kin system, however, slaves were trusted more than kith and kin. As soldiers and officials, slaves often wielded authority over free Muslims. Freed African slaves developed personal skills which they could not have gained if they had remained in Africa.

The Islamic concept of slavery was based on the legal status of bondage concerning three categories of slaves—domestic, laboring, and military. Pipes (1981) points out that slaves were not necessarily poor, politically subjugated, or of low social status. Islam clearly identifies who a slave is and the humanity of the slave is recognized. However, a slave is not permitted to perform the *Hajj* alone and must be accompanied by a master. Islamic laws are quite explicit as to what a slave cannot be subjected to. For example, a concubine should be set free when her master dies, and if she bore her master's children (who were free), she could not be sold.

The slave trade transferred ownership of one human being to another (a master or mistress), who thereby acquired rights regarding the slave's marriage, renting or subletting their services to others, in order to earn monetary returns. Saunders (1982) remarks that slaves were branded and shipped from Guinea—and then they were rebranded after each resale. The Portuguese branded slaves on their arms; other masters were less kind and even had their slaves branded on their cheeks.

The slave traders ignored ethical issues over and above those of slavery. Within postcolonial nations, slaves brought by European colonizers were forgotten and consigned to an ethical vacuum. Western scholars have concentrated on the transatlantic slave trade at the cost of excluding other important African migrations. The views of indigenous Asian scholars remain little known, though much value has been placed on insider stories recently.

The captives of Africa's internal wars were either enslaved within Africa or sold to the Muslim East and India. African ivory was the most sought after commodity by Indians, and it was carried by slaves to the coast, where both the ivory and slaves were sold. When the demand for labor increased, trading in human cargo became more profitable than ivory.

The slave trade resulted in Africans being kidnapped, sold or shipped to unfamiliar territories. The ethnic origins of the Africans were unimportant to the slavers who were simply dealing with human cargo. As a result, it is difficult to pinpoint the exact place of a slave's origin or tribe. Also, conversion to Islam or Christianity, even on board the ships sailing from Africa to Asian ports, complicates the picture since slaves often abandoned their names in favor of Arabic or Western names. Unfortunately, this name change also meant that valuable information about their tribal origins was lost. It should be noted that the Trinidadi Muslims, who signed a petition for repatriation to Africa in 1838, recorded both their original Arabic names and the new western names that they were given after forced conversion to Christianity: Salhiu (Charles Alexander), Mahammed Waatra (Auguste Bernard), Mahommed Habia (Mahommed Littledale), Mahommed Sissei (Felix Ditt), Fonta Torre (Sampson Boissier), Abouberika Torre (Joseph Sampson), Brahima (Adam Balthasar), Hammadi Torrouke (Louis Modeste), Mahommed Balliah (Christopher Picka), Samba Jaiih (Michael Sylvestre) and Malick Job (Thomas Jones) (Trotman and Lovejoy 2004:221). This illustrates how migrants wanted to retain their ethnic identity through their names. Most of this information is unavailable for trans-Indian Oceanic African slaves due to the many centuries that slavery prevailed, and the lack of documented historical accounts.

Western slavery was based on the commodification of human beings. Ultimately, the contradiction between this and the economic idea of freedom within a capitalistic labor market undermined its economic rationale. This would have been true even in the absence of moral and humanitarian arguments. Eric Williams (1944:169) states that "capitalism had first encouraged West Indian slavery and then helped to destroy it. When British capitalism depended on the West Indies, they ignored slavery or defended it. When British capitalism found the West Indian monopoly a nuisance, they destroyed West Indian slavery as the first step in the destruction of the West Indian monopoly."

Patterns of Slavery

Eastward migration is a neglected area of research on the long-standing movement of Africans. While migrations across the Atlantic were widespread from 1440 to 1870, Red Sea and Indian Ocean crossings had carried on for a few millennia. In the 1970s, the African-American historian, Joseph Harris, drew attention to other areas of African migration. While commenting on the need to explore the history of Afro-Asians, he told me, "It's up to you now: you speak their languages." Joseph Harris acknowledges the limitations of exploring these issues from the perspective of a single discipline, ethnic group or nation. These comments were made at a conference organized by UNESCO in Paris (2004) to "Commemorate the Struggle against Slavery and its Abolition"; I was the only scholar researching the Indian Ocean diaspora who was invited to read a paper at the conference. The task of breaking the code is essential to the need for local participation. Asians have an advantage in writing the story of African migrants because they have the necessary communication skills to interact with contemporary Afro-Asian communities. Moreover, the Africans, after all the past centuries, have become Asians. From a physiognomical point of view, only curly hair differentiates them. Historians tend to get lost in facts and figures. At a UNESCO conference held in 1978, Hubert Gerbeau (1979:184–207) reminded historians that "dating the cargoes and counting the men and the piasters" was insufficient. He reminded historians attempting to analyze the African diasporas that they would also have to be archaeologists, ethnologists, specialists in oral tradition, biologists, linguists, and perhaps psychiatrists.

My attempts at getting to the roots of the Afro-Sri Lankans led me to the Ethiopianist Richard Pankhurst. Realizing that there may be isolated researchers working on dispersed Africans, we decided to approach scholars for articles about twelve years ago. It was difficult to find scholars; some had little time to write articles and others lacked adequate material. Yet, we were fortunate to have on board Edward Alpers (University of California, Los Angeles), Eduardo Medeiros (University of Evora, Portugal), Malyn Newitt (King's College London, U.K.), Jean Houbert (University of Aberdeen, Scotland), Helen Hintjens (University of Swansea, Wales), and Helene Basu (Free University, Germany). Altogether, we published a collection of eight articles that brought to light something of the African presence in the Indian Ocean. Kassahun Checole, Managing Director of Africa World Press, agreed to publish our book, entitled *The African Diaspora in the Indian Ocean* (de Silva Jayasuriya 2003a; de Silva Jayasuriya and Pankhurst 2003). It was obvious that much more work remained to be done.

From documented commercial contacts and ongoing trade between Africa and Asia, we know that there were voluntary migrants. A large number of migrants were, however, victims of the slave trade. The history of Africans and Asians, therefore, is inevitably tied in with slavery and the slave trade. Indigenous systems of slavery and servitude existed, but in the event of displacement from one continent to another, the slave was inevitably an outsider. Slaves were therefore without kinship ties and landless. As the property of a master or mistress, the slave could be sold to another. The slave trade reduced human beings to the status of a commodity that could be bought and sold. The prices of female, male and child slaves varied across time and space, reflecting their changing demand in various places and at different times.

Slaves in the Middle East were not only black; some were white as well. Circassians from Asia Minor were prized slaves (Lewis 1971). In the pecking order for African slaves, Abyssinians were the most desired, probably because of their lighter skin color.

The labor demand for agricultural work in lower Iraq, together with the rise in international commerce in the Indian Ocean, stimulated the slave trade. African migration to Asia peaked when the European nations battled to gain control of the East. However, intra-Asian and African-Asian commerce existed before the Portuguese made their entrance to the Indian Ocean in the fifteenth century. Arab domination of Indian Ocean trade from about the sixth century and then the spread of Islam together with trading contacts from the eighth century onwards stimulated African migration.

Although it is often viewed as a western cultural attribute, Christianity was not introduced to the East by the European colonizers. Consequently, Africans who converted to Christianity were associated with the European colonial machinery. After decolonization, the fate of Christian Africans who remained in Asia began to change. In some instances, such as in Sri Lanka, this change began during colonial rule when the demand for African soldiers fell due to the political stability and economic constraints of the empire. In this respect, Afro-Asians are similar to the Euro-Asians. Indeed, Afro-Asians are often associated with Europeans by the indigenous Asians.

Lovejoy (2004b:239) points out that in the Americas enslaved Muslims were almost exclusively young males. He adds that 95% of those enslaved from the Central Sudan in the eighteenth and nineteenth centuries were males. This was also true for Western Sudan. However, in contrast, the general pattern of transatlantic slavery involved an equal number of males and females (Eltis 1986). Significantly, the Muslim slaves in the Americas have varied backgrounds and lives of captivity. Several were from military and aristocratic elite families, which led them to seek emancipation on the grounds that they should never have been enslaved as freeborn Muslims. The story of Ayuba Suleiman Diallo of Futa Bundu, who was called Job ben Solomon by the Europeans, was published in 1734; it received much publicity and was translated into French.

African Migrants: A New Perspective

Eastward migrants served in both the service and defense sectors. They were mostly "forms of consumption" unlike the Atlantic migrants who became "factors of production." Westward migrants were economically exploited—and this affected their process of assimilation into the host society. Also, the skin color problem impinged on African Americans who had to travel with European migrants to the New World. In Asia, Africans assimilated more easily, as color was less of a problem; the skin color of indigenous Asians varies.

The emphasis on slavery and the slave trade as social and economic institutions carries certain risks. Scholars tend to ignore the African contribution to Asian societies. Assimilation has led to a blurring of "African-ness" and migrants have lost their "otherness." Even though Afro-Asians tend to be associated with slavery and marginalization, it is important to recognize that elite Africans live in India today. I have met descendants of the royal Africans in Janjira and Sachin who consider their African heritage prestigious. It is apparent that the fate of all African migrants was not the same (see Chapter 6).

Examining the fate of African migrants calls for open-mindedness. The tendency is to judge all migrations by the more widely known fate of African Americans. Africans reached high positions of leadership that indigenous Asians were unable to achieve since their status changed from outsider to insider within a few years of living in India. These processes of social mobility underline the complexity and variety of Asian societies.

Africans were displaced to lands across the Indian Ocean, up to the shores of China and Japan, and therefore into the Pacific. These migrations have been overshadowed by the current focus on commemorating the bicentennial of the abolition of the transatlantic slave trade. On the other hand, the bicentennial has aroused contemporary interest in involuntary African migration and the status of its victims.

The routes of African migrations across the Red Sea and the Indian Ocean varied, often indicating the economic networks established at the time that the slaves were bought and sold in local markets (see Chapter 3). Africans were thrown into host societies that were not homogeneous and differed in religion, language, and other cultural aspects.

Perhaps the similarities between the transatlantic and transindian Oceanic migrants lie in the musical traditions that have been maintained. In some cases, these traditions entered the mainstream culture. Once again, one sees a difference here: the African contribution to the music of the Americas and the world has gained a high profile. In this respect, the Atlantic world has been more receptive to African-influenced music, perhaps because new migrants were part of the higher stratas of society. Cultural flows to the non-Africans, especially among the elite and middle classes, were more effective in the West. Hybridized or altered forms of African music were adopted and marketed by those with European ancestry, adding a touch of social acceptance. Genres that originated among African slaves became popular forms of music in the Americas and beyond, even spilling into the Asian world, due to colonization. Yet the African-influenced genres in the East are not globally known and often barely recognized even locally.

Religious conversions and transformation of cultural values stimulated the process of assimilation into the new host societies. This is particularly true for those who converted to Islam and to a lesser degree for those who became Christians. As the migrants remained in Islamic societies and became part of those communities, their ethnic origins became less important to the hosts. In addition, their origins surfaced through cultural expressions, particularly music and dance. This is evident in popular and religious music and in spirit possession rituals that are carried out by African peoples (Chapter 5).

Another reason for the lack of scholarship or general awareness of the African presence in Asia is the existence of numerous ethnonyms that have been used throughout time and space. Given that *Africa* is a twentieth-century term, understandably, people from its continent were and are still called by various ethnonyms. Previously, black Africans were perceived to have come from the Sudan, the Habasha, the Zandj or the Nuba. The medieval Arab chronicler, Al-Idrisi (1100–1162) recorded that Ghana was "the greatest country in the land of the Sudan, the most populous, and having most extensive trade" (Levtzion 1977:349). Ghana and Sudan are two distinct countries which are on opposite sides of the continent today.

Segal (2001:3) remarks that the Islamic trade was conducted on a different scale and had a different impact. The social and cultural impact of Islamic slavery was greater than the economic benefits gained. Slaves, as concubines, porters, soldiers or cooks, worked in the service sector. While more females were affected by Islamic slavery, more male slaves were forced to move across the Atlantic. This does not hold as a general rule. At certain times, within the same country, males were in demand. In some Indian Ocean countries, as for example in Sri Lanka, the population census statistics show equal numbers of African men and women, at least in the period for which census statistics are available. The census records of Sri Lanka taken at ten yearly intervals, from 1871 to 1921, show nearly an equal number of female and male *Kaffirs* (the ethnonym for Africans in Sri Lanka, which is a colonial carryover) during the 50 years for which population statistics are available. There were 245 Kaffirs (132 males and 113 females) in 1871; 408 Kaffirs (204 males and 204 females) in 1881; 405 Kaffirs (214 males and 191 females) in 1891; 318 Kaffirs (166 males and 152 females) in 1901; 253 Kaffirs (132 males and 121 females) in 1911; and 255 (138 males and 117 females) in 1921. Afro-Sri Lankans have not appeared in the population census as a separate ethnic group since 1911. They now appear in the "Others" category, which includes small minorities (de Silva Jayasuriya 2006a).

Three forms of slavery have been identified in the subcontinent by Sarkar (1985): first, an urban, market-oriented system where slaves were like chattel, being bought and sold; secondly, a traditional system of domestic slavery which was limited to a local supply; and thirdly, an agrestic or praedial slavery in which a slave was tied to the low caste status. Her suggestions need further investigation, taking into account the societies in the regions loosely bound by caste divisions.

In India, African slave-soldiers gained military control and power in the Bengal Sultante, Deccan Plateau, and Gujarat Sultanate during the fifteenth and sixteenth centuries. African contributions to the host societies have been quite conspicuous in some instances. In India, Malik Ambar, who became the Regent Minister of Ahmednagar in the Deccan, is undoubtedly the best known in Indian history. However, he was not the only African to reach the corridors of power in India. The depictions of Africans in Indian art establish the African presence when written records are scarce (Robbins and McLeod 2006). Chapter 4 draws attention to the military contributions of Africans to Asia.

Oral traditions fill a gap in the literature, and it is important to record histories and folklore before valuable information is lost. While Afro-Asians had no political voice, their musical traditions remain vibrant today. In Chapter 5, I put forward the hypothesis that music and dance have been maintained among African migrants and their descendants, even though they may have lost other cultural elements, such as language and religion. African migrants act as cultural brokers between Africa and Asia. Cultural flows between Africa and Asia, particularly music, need to be brought to the fore. The lyrics of Afro-Asian songs remain an indispensible database, exposing African linguistic links. The rhythms of the songs indicate multiple origins or exposure to several styles of music—both African and Asian—en route to a new destination. The musical abilities of the Afro-Asians need to be nurtured and brought to national and international stages. Afro-Asians need a market-maker, as their music is internationally marketable. Flows of music to the host countries are also not well recognized. Having mapped African musical traditions in Asia, I have discovered that in some cases these musical traditions have moved into the mainstream culture, becoming the most popular genres of music today. Perhaps the irresistible rhythms of African music contributed to this unexpected outcome.

Africans were forced to live in societies with other cultural values, creating problems—not least linguistically. The languages they needed to speak would have depended on their work in Asia. Perhaps importantly, Africans were also interpreters for the European expansionists, reflecting their multilinguality.

Chanting, controlled breathing, and rhythmic bodily movements, which led to trances and spirit possessions, were common practices in East African coastal towns and even on the Arab *dhows* (a traditional sailing vessel) which transported slaves to be sold. By studying musical traditions and lyrics of the diaspora, one might expect to be able to forge links with traditions in Africa, which might shed some light on the ethnicity of the slaves. By taking into account different Afro-Asian living conditions and by making comparisons, one can build a more comprehensive picture than what would be possible if the focus were simply on a single community.

All markets are demand-driven, and the slave trade could not have survived without the demand for slaves. Even after Abolition, the slave trade continued surreptitiously. Abolition did not end slavery completely. Since the slave trade affected the hinterlands and the littoral, any future research centered on villages, ocean basins and maritime life should shed new light on global history and on the slave trade itself.

Religious values influenced Eastern slavery which was service-oriented. Africans were placed in ancient and pluralistic societies. The impact of the color factor was diluted because some indigenous Asians were as dark-skinned as Africans. Moreover, considerable miscegenation among Africans and Asians resulted in offspring who became part of the kin system.

At times, the slave trade was conducted brutally, and in some places the ethical issues—or what we now call human rights—were ignored. Within many former colonies, the participation of European powers in the trade which caused long-distance displacement of Africans has been forgotten. Consequently, the slave trade is neither a historical nor an ethical issue.

It is noteworthy that scholars generally tend to disregard the African contributions to their societies. Susana Baca (UNESCO Newsletter 2004:25), the Peruvian soloist, voiced her opinion at the UNESCO conference held in Paris to mark the International Year to Commemorate the Struggle against Slavery and the Abolition: "There is a need to promote research and assessment of the contribution of African cultures to the world, to share and disseminate such knowledge widely. What traces has the slave left on his or her route, and what has been his or her contribution"?

Baca's remarks perfectly summarize the problem facing historians, social scientists and policymakers, bringing to the surface the task of writing the history of silence. As a musician, I share Susana Baca's sentiments about the cultural contributions that the Africans have left behind, and the need to bring these aspects to the fore. Therefore, in addition to drawing attention to contemporary Afro-Asian communities, this book also brings to the fore the role of African migrants as cultural brokers of African music, dance, and song within Asian societies.

In the Atlantic model, the African slave became a "factor of production" in a triangular trade that involved three continents. African slaves worked on American plantations and mines, producing goods that were shipped across the Atlantic to Europe. For Asia there is no single model. First, Africans moved voluntarily to the East. Secondly, the length of time over which involuntary migration occurred and the lack of historical detail make an analysis more complicated. Thirdly, the people involved in the slave trade at various times and their motives for requiring Africans varied. Fourthly, the diversity of the host societies in languages, religions, food, clothing, customs, music, and dance as well as the extent of assimilation and marginalization complicate the study of Africans in the East today. In this book, I will illustrate that Africans who moved eastward were more service providers than they were plantation workers. As a result, they came into closer contact with Asians. The variety of tasks that Africans performed in Asia—sailors, soldiers, bodyguards, commanders, domestic servants, nannies, musicians, entertainers, and interpreters—brought them into close proximity with their hosts. No doubt, this affected the extent of assimilation, integration, and marginalization. Learning new Asian languages or lingua franca helped the slaves adjust to an alien cultural matrix. Even so, Africans held on to their religious beliefs, expressing them through spirit possession ceremonies. They were able to maintain something of their musical traditions, even reproducing their sense of rhythm by making instruments in their new homes. In a subtle way, they acted as cultural brokers between Africa and Asia, sometimes even becoming the interface between the traditions of three continents as initiators of new musical genres that have been absorbed into postcolonial nations.

CHAPTER 2

The African Presence in Asia

The eastward movement of Africans from Turkey to Japan has received little attention from academics and policymakers. Is this because these Africans have lacked a voice? How can one write the history of the subaltern? Historical records contain few references to Africans in Asia. Therefore, we need to take oral histories into account. However, since many generations of Africans were born in Asia, memories are patchy and tend to be a mixture of facts that have been learned from those outside their community, along with oral traditions that have been handed down by their forebears.

Assimilation, largely through intermarriage, has made it difficult to distinguish Africans from other ethnic groups in Asia. Successful assimilation contributes to the problem of identifying Asians with African ancestry today. Perhaps too much pressure has been placed upon historians to try and reveal the African presence in Asia. A historian who depends on archival sources—logbooks, traveler's accounts, court records, treaties, customs documents, and shipping documents—would be unable to identify Africans since Arabic or Christian names that were adopted after conversion would generally be recorded. The African presence was concealed by conversion to Islam or Christianity. Generally, Africans would be indistinguishable from the Arabs by name. Therefore, Portuguese documents from the sixteenth century, the British East India Company's records from the seventeenth century, and any Dutch and French material would be of limited value.

Histories based on memory, such as oral history and ethnohistory, are now established disciplines (Fentress and Wickham 1992). Oral history includes mythology, genealogy, and narrative history. An individual's recollections, often the focus of oral histories, are limited to a person's experiences and exposures. People are generally able to distinguish between personal memories and oral traditions—what is recounted, sometimes by professionals, of a past that is too remote to have been experienced by its narrators, or sometimes as with folktales, of a past that is recognized as imaginary.

Memory can also be treated as a text and a receptacle of information. Historians have developed a method of analyzing oral text and correlating it with written documents and other pieces of information. With reasonable certainty, historians can "restore" oral text to its "original" form and situate it within its social context, thereby establishing the particular perspective on the past that the "oral document" puts forth. As historians more or less consciously formulate interpretations of the past, which they use to structure their material, historical records are not, in principle, different from oral accounts. Unless a society can freeze the memory of the past, it tends to suppress what is not meaningful or intuitively satisfying in the collective memories of the past, interpolating or substituting what seems more appropriate or in keeping with its particular conception of the world. Often constructed through myths and literature, collective memory plays an important role in creating the identity of migrant communities. Historians tend to question the validity of oral histories and recollections of the past, assuming that history is scientific. They have been able to convince learned societies that the facts represented by professional historians are the truth. Increasingly, historical records have been viewed as biased, illustrating that the historians make their own subjective value judgements and distorts them while reading documents. Historians have reinterpreted the past and presented it to learned society as the gospel truth. It takes a long time to change society's views of history and get it to accept the relevance and importance of oral accounts. Moreover, once an oral account is documented, it becomes a historical document.

Even though historians have worked out a methodology to analyze oral history, most of their research is still based on written records. Oral history is a new and relatively recent source of information, and it has its own problems. One cannot expect to find information in documented and tangible records for those who are disenfranchised. Most historians overlook the people of African descent who live in Asia as well as their special circumstances within these countries. African history is oral, and Afro-Asians have many stories about how they came to live in Asia today. There have been several migratory waves to Asia, with Africans originating from various locations and perhaps even spending some time in one Asian country before being taken to another country in the East.

While contextualizing African migration within a chronological framework, one should keep in mind the drawbacks of archival documents. Migration has caused problems with kinship and alliance—and it has created legal and economic problems. An anthropologist, who studies a single community, may make observations and inferences that are limited since the focus is only on one community. This chapter illustrates the movement of Africans and African communities in the East.

Eastward migration of Africans has gone on for about two millennia. Moreover, whole or parts of the continent's name have changed throughout the centuries of migration under review in this book. Firstly, it is important to draw attention to the various names in the literature that are used throughout the centuries and even today for Afro-Asians. These ethnonyms were used for enslaved and freed Africans and also for descendants of freed African slaves.

During medieval times, Africans were perceived as coming from a particular geographical area on the continent and were therefore referred to by the name given to that region. People of tropical Africa belonged to the Sudan, the Habasha, the Zandj, or the Nuba. *As-sudan* is the plural of the Arabic word *al-aswad* meaning "black." *Bilad al-Sudan* (land of the blacks) or Sudan was the area south of the Maghrib. The term *Habasha/ Habashi/Habshi* (Abyssinians or Ethiopians) was well known, as it was geographically closer to Arabia. A prominent African tribe that settled in Arabia was called *Habashan*. The East African coast was called *Zandj*. In the fourteenth century, Ibn Batuta, the Moroccan traveler, referred to the Swahili Coast as *Bilad al Zanj* (land of the Zanj). Following the conquest of Egypt, Nuba and its people became known to the Arabs.

People of African descent in South Asia have mostly been referred to as Habshi, Kaffir, and *Sidi*. All these words have Arabic etyma. The Habshi were associated with Prophet Muhammad. Bilal, the first *mu'ad-hdhin* (one who calls Muslims to prayer), was the son of an Ethiopian slave. Many historians called enslaved Africans in India *Habshi*, a term that encompassed East Africans, from the Horn of Africa to Mozambique (Burton-Page 1971).

Kaffir is from the Arabic word *qafr* meaning "non-believer" and was originally used to refer to those who were not Muslims. For example, in Calcutta (India), Africans were called Coffrey (a variation of Kaffir): "Run Away from on board of a Vessel, A Coffrey [African] slave boy, about five feet high, named Anthony" (*The India Gazette and Calcutta Public Advertiser* 1786). Chattopadhyay (1963:74), for example, refers to the 1820s when the price of *coffree* slaves was high—they had a rarity value, but even Indian slaves were more expensive in Calcutta than in other parts of Bengal. Chattopadhyay (1963) examined slavery in the Bengal presidency under East India Company rule between 1772 and 1843. At that time, slaves were marketable commodities in every district of the Bengal Presidency, and buying and selling slaves was permitted by law.

The etymon of the word *Sidi* is from Arabic *Seyidi/Sayeedi/Sayedi* meaning "lord or master." Sidi was used as an honorific title, like Sidi Yaqut, for example. In the nineteenth-century Indian Ocean, the British called African seamen, both enslaved and freed, *Seedies* (Ewald 2000:83). Nowadays, many Afro-Indians use Sidi as a surname or family identifier (for example, Mohamed Hussein Sidi or Sidi Hajif Ganibhai).

For example, Camara (2004:102) mentions that Afro-Indians are called Sidi, Habshi, *Kaphri, Shamal, Badsha, Landa* and *Kafira*, in various languages such as Marathi, Kannada, Konkani, Gujarati, Telugu, and Urdu. In this book, the term *Afro-Indian* will be used for people in India of African descent. Some scholars have implied that Habshis began to call themselves Sidis after some years in India. They also associate the word *Sidi* with Muslim Africans, suggesting that the etymon of Sidi is *Sayyid* (from the Arabic word which means that they have descended from the Prophet Muhammed).

Middle East

Migrants are an important component of the Middle Eastern population. In multiethnic Turkey, Africans, who were brought by the Ottoman Turks to the Mediterranean city of Antalya, have received little attention. Planhil (1958:350-371) has drawn attention to the mixed ethnicity of Turkey and the presence of Africans. Descendants of Africans, who were brought to Turkey during the Ottoman Empire, contribute to its diversity today. In 1847, the Ottoman Sultan closed the slave market in Constantinople and stopped importing slaves through the Persian Gulf. Durugonul (2003:282) points out that studies on Afro-Turks are limited; she also remarks that the search for a national identity hampers social integration. Multiculturalism and plural identities conflict with political and ideological views that emphasize a Turkish-Islamic and Ottoman history. If the society is unaware of how, why and when it became heterogeneous, it cannot cope with multiculturalism. The first step to pluralism, then, is a new historiography that acknowledges African migration and the reasons behind it. A politically-immobilized community that lacks an awareness of their African ancestry has further problematized this dilemma.

According to the customs register, male and female black slaves were the major exports that were loaded onto ships in Egypt sailing to Antalya (Inalcik and Quataert 1994:285). Segal (2001:114) points out that the black slaves went to other Anatolian cities such as Bursa. In Turkey, Anatolia was a major African slave market. Some African slaves came on steamers through Egypt and others were brought by land from Baghdad. In December 1889, the sultan issued a "law for the repression of the Negro Slave-Trade in the Ottoman Empire" (British Sessional Papers 1889).

Sudanese and Nubians were brought to Palestine as slaves but others migrated and even formed their own villages. During the British mandate, many worked as domestic servants, guards, and snack sellers. Many of their descendants still live in Israel/Palestine and have been absorbed into communities. They now speak Palestinian Arabic and intermarry with Arabs. Beckerleg (2007) researched the African Bedouin in Palestine (Chapter 6).

Since the beginning of the twentieth century, Ethiopian Jews/*Falashas* have been coming to Israel, but most of them immigrated in the 1980s. Tens of thousands of them live in contemporary Israel. They were previously called *Falashas;* however, the term is now considered pejorative and no longer in use. Since at least the nineteenth century, Ethiopian Christians have been a community in Jerusalem. Even today, there is a street called Ethiopia Street, formerly called the Ethiopians' Street because mostly Ethiopians lived there. There are several Ethiopian churches and monasteries in Jerusalem. Many recent immigrants, known as *Falashmuras*, are Ethiopian Christians who claim to be descendants of Jews. Black Hebrews are part of a community which immigrated to Israel in the 1970s from the United States. They claimed to be "the original Jews," but have since abandoned these claims. Most of them came to Israel as tourists. The Israeli government decided to give them permanent resident status in July 2003. Several thousands of Black Hebrews now live in Israel, mainly in the southern town of Dimona (Tadmor 2005:personal communication).

An Israeli government's policy that allowed migrant workers into the country resulted in Ghanaians and Nigerians arriving in the late 1980s (Sabar and Shlomit 2006). Educated to tertiary level in their countries, many of these migrants were motivated by the economic enhancements that they could gain by working outside their home countries even in jobs that were beneath their level of education. They came without work visas but were able to find work in Israel. Many Africans came on pilgrimages and entered Israel on tourist visas. The first Africans, who came to Israel in the late 1980s, created the platform for others to follow by building up contacts and learning the ropes. By the end of the 1990s, an estimated number of 10,000 to 14,000 Africans lived in Israel (Kemp and Reichman 2003).

The largest number of African slaves lived in Iraq during the eighth century, and perhaps not surprisingly, this led to one of the bloodiest revolts in Islamic history (Lombard 1971:153). Between the eighth and nineth centuries, several Bantu-speaking Africans, whom the Arabs called the *Zanj*, were traded to Iraq where they worked in salt marshes. During that time, Iraq had the highest concentration of black slaves. There were a series of revolts against the Abbasid Empire (762–1258)— and the longest lasted from 869 to 883. During the Zanj rebellion, Bantu, Sudanese, Nubian and local slaves organized themselves into a large army and occupied Iraqi cities. They even built their own capital. The military skills exhibited by the Africans during the Zanj rebellion increased the interest among Arab rulers for recruiting African soldiers (Chapter 4).

Mirzai (2005:30) draws attention to the forced migration from the peripheries of the Islamic world—that is, the Steppes of southern Russia and Africa to the Middle East. She adds that eastern and northeastern Africans were brought to Iran, while West Africans were taken to the Ottoman world. Many slaves in the littoral of the Persian Gulf served as pearl fishers, domestics and laborers. Domestics were in demand in Baluchistan as well as in the cities. Agricultural laborers worked in Baluchistan while the African eunuchs served in the harems. There were both male and female (wet and dry) nurses. Afro-Iranian communities exist along the shores of the Persian Gulf, but they integrated themselves into certain areas (for example, in Shiraz). Mirzai (2005:32), however, points out that Afro-Iranian communities and their culture continue to prevail in southern Iran. Small African settlements were discovered in *Zanjiabad* (a village built by Africans), *Gala-Zanjian* (Castle of Africans), near the "Mount of the Blacks" in Baluchistan, and *Deh-Zanjian* (a village built by Africans) in Kerman Province. Slaves from the *Zanj* (Kenyans and Tanzanians) were brought to Khūzistān as laborers to work in the sugar plantations (Hunwick 1978:25).

In 936, twelve thousand African slaves were traded by an Iranian trader (Ricks 1988:3). In Bam, the presence of several hundred African slaves was reported in the fifteenth century (Aubin 1956:92, 94).

In 1877, the main financial officer of Isfahan reported that a large number of slaves were living there. Some were freed; however, the majority were *khaneshad* (children of slaves). At a time when the sale of slaves flourished, many were brought to Isfahan and sold. Most of them had married among themselves. However, after some years, the sale of

slaves was forbidden. Nevertheless, a few slaves were still brought to
Isfahan from Ethiopia and Zanzibar (Segal 2001:126). Harris (1971:77-
78) located a separate black community near Jiruft, which was a trading
place for goods and Africans. They had spoken a language that was not
understood by other Iranians. Another black community had lived near
Bandar Abbas and were descendants of Africans employed on *dhows* or
date plantations. Slaves bought by Iranian Muslims in Arabia while on
pilgrimage were brought back to Shiraz where no community of Africans
existed.

Slave Market in Zanzibar
(Source: Richard Howard, *Black Cargo*.
London: Wayland Publishers, 1972)

According to Khalifa (2006a:61), the African presence in Dubai remains vibrant in the *zar* or spirit possession ceremonies. She draws attention to African slaves in Dubai and the Gulf, who have left their mark through practices of zar. The *tanburah* (lyre), an instrument that is central to spirit possession ceremonies in the Gulf, is important because it brings to the surface the African roots of some people in the Gulf. In both Africa and Gulf communities, lyre use is considered a marginal survival by ethnomusicologists. In other words, it is a tradition or artefact that can be found mainly in the geographical peripheries of its place of origin (Racy 1992:7–17).

Alpers (2004a:29) notes that changes in the demand for labor were triggered by the industrial revolution in Europe and America and its effects in the Middle East. Firstly, the port cities of the Arabian Peninsula created an increase in the demand for labor, which was met from the northeastern and eastern Africa. Secondly, the expansion of the date plantations in the Persian Gulf required labor; this further stimulated African enslavement. Thirdly, the demand for workers at the pearl industry in the Red Sea and the Persian Gulf was met from Africa as well.

Alpers (2004b:57) mentions the existence of a large African slave population due to the Busaidi control of Zanzibar. In the last part of the nineteenth century, according to a French naval officer, freed slaves were about 25% of the Omani population (Germain 1868:351).

In the nineteenth century, Somali and Nubian slaves were born in the Hadramaut (South Yemen). Freed slaves often preferred to migrate to Indonesia in search of employment, which suggests that people of African descent live in Indonesia today, other than those left behind by the Black Dutchmen (*Orang Belinda Hitam*) mentioned later on. The British had set up a colony in Aden for freed slaves. According to Serjeant, slaves who found their way to the Aden colony were apparently set free (1987). Harold Ingrams, the first British Commissioner to the Qu'aiti Sultanate (1942:349) who served from 1934 to 1944, discovered 4,000 to 5,000 people, mostly of African descent, who were free but in a technical state of slavery. The Akhdam, Yemenis of African origin, lived and worked outside the traditional tribal structure (Ingrams 2006:71), with dwellings beyond the walls of large cities. The Hajur and Subians in Yemen are also of African origin. All these people, who are probably descendants of Abyssinians, were laborers, both agricultural and casual, sweepers, and fishermen.

South Asia

Baptiste (2006) draws attention to the presence of Africans in Afghanistan. We have not been able to ascertain if there are people of African descent in Afghanistan today, but the *Account of the Kingdom of Caubul*, written by Mountstuart Elphinstone and published in 1815, mentions Africans living there in the early nineteenth century. Elphinstone served the British East India Company—and subsequently, the British Raj between 1796 and 1826. He was sent to Kabul on a diplomatic mission that involved a reported plan by Napoleon in Egypt to launch an attack on the British Empire in India, in alliance with the Ottoman Turk and Persian empires. Therefore, historical evidence suggests that Habshis served in the courts of Kabul during the early nineteenth century.

In Pakistan, there are a large number of people with African ancestry. Given the strategic importance of the Makran coast in Balochistan, which was on the trade route to and from Africa, Arabia, Central Asia, and South Asia, it is not surprising that African slaves may have traveled on this route as well. As early as the third century, Omani Arabs settled on the Makran coast and became important slave dealers and middlemen, feeding the South Asian demand. Although they have been referred to by several names—*gulam* (slave), *naukar* (servant/slave), *dada* (black), *shidi* (black), and *syah* (black)—I found that they are simply known as Makranis to many Indians and Pakistani, as they are associated with their coastal dwellings. Toponyms such as Mombasa Street and Sheedi Village Road in Karachi consolidate the African connection to Pakistan (Badalkhan 2006). Burton (1992) provides the details of the Africans who lived in the mid-nineteenth century in Sindh, now a province of Pakistan (see Chapter 6).

In the nearby Maldive Islands, two mechanisms for African migration are evident. First, Africans were brought as slaves on Arab dhows. In 1834, two British naval lieutenants, who visited Male, reported that "from the information we were able to collect—it appears that Muscat vessels do not often visit this place: when they do, they generally bring a cargo of slaves. Five years ago, one came and sold about twenty-five lads, at an average price of about 80 rupees each" (Forbes and Ali 1980:19). Secondly, sultans returning from the Hajj brought back slaves who were eventually freed on conversion. Freed slaves assimilated into the Maldivian population which was historically accustomed to migrant settlers. Africans intermarried with the indigenous Maldivians. Most Africans worked as *raveris* or coconut plantation keepers—and this suggests an existing shortage of labor supply.

In Maldives, natural resources and commodities include coir, cowry shells, ambergris and dry fish. The Maldives have traded with Persians, Arabs, Malays, Indians and Sri Lankans. Since its commercial potential was low compared to some of its neighbors, Maldives was not the immediate focus of western traders and colonizers. It, however, established itself as a place for repairing ships, mainly because the coir in the Maldives was of good quality. (The fibers of the many coconut trees that abound in the islands are converted into coir rope.) Maldivian cowrie shells were considered the best in the world due to their whiteness. They were, however, more than just a commodity–they were also monetary units.

The Portuguese got entangled in the Maldives because of their struggle with Mamale of Kannanur, South India. They had a brief presence (1558–1573) in the Maldives. Coir rope made from coconut fiber was sought after in all of Asia. The early sixteenth-century Portuguese chronicler, João de Barros, wrote that "the commonest and most important merchandise at these islands, indeed, the cause of them being visited, is the coir; without it, those seas cannot be navigated" (de Barros 1638).

Besides commerce and colonization, other phenomena led to African migration. Some Africans were destined to live in faraway lands because they were purchased by pilgrims from many parts of the world in markets at Mecca and Medina. In the Maldives, Africans have been called

Habshi, Baburu, and Sidi but not Kaffir. The word Habshi, from the Arabic word al-Habash, referred to an Abyssinian (or Ethiopian) at that time. It may have been a generic term used for all Africans who were believed to have come from a single geographical entity. The Moroccan traveler Ibn Batuta visited the Habshigefanu (shrine of an African Saint in the Maldives), which implies that Africans were key religious figures within Islam in the fourteenth century.

According to the Anthropological Survey of India (1996), Afro-Indian communities can be found in southern India (Andhra Pradesh and Karnataka), western India (Gujarat) and in the cities of Delhi, Kolkata (Calcutta), and Mumbai (Bombay). Since then, Afro-Indians have also been reported in Goa. There are Christian, Hindu, and Muslim Afro-Indians. This is in contrast to neighboring Sri Lanka, where most Africans have been Christians, demonstrating that we cannot judge the entire Indian subcontinent in the same way.

Africans either lived or currently reside in the Indian states of Andhra Pradesh, Bengal, Bihar, Goa, Gujarat, Karnataka, Kerala, Maharashtra, Madya Pradesh, Tamil Nadu, Uttar Pradesh, and West Bengal. Some scholars have suggested that after slavery was abolished in Portuguese India during the mid-nineteenth century, most freedmen fled from Goa to the western Ghats, where their descendants can be found living in small communities today. There are communities in the neighboring state of Karnataka in Yellapur, Halliyal, Ankola, and Mundgod Peta (Bouketo 2006:161). In addition, there are communities in Uttara Kannada, Dharwar, and Belgaum.

In the Maharashtra State, Indians of African descent were reported in Kolhapur, Raigarh, Bombay, and Thana. During the nineteenth century, Africans lived near the Bombay prison and had their own quarters. In Gujarat, they can be found in Kutch, Jamnagar, Portbander, Junagadh, Amreli, Bhavnagar, Rajkot, Ratanpur, Surendranagar, Ahmedabad, Surat, Saurashtra, Bharuch, Daman, and Diu.

Omar Khalidi (2006:248) dates the African settlement in Hyderabad to at least the early sixteenth century, during the reign of Sultan Quli Qutb Shah, who was the first Sultan of Golconda. He conjectures that it may have been even earlier, from the time of the Bahmani Sultanate, which began in 1347 with Hasan Gangu as the first Bahmani Sultan. The second sultan of the Bahmani Sulanate, Taj du-Din Firus Shah, was murdered by his African bodyguards.

In 1882 the Indian government began to control the migration of Africans to Hyderabad, believing that they consorted with the Arab migrants from Hadramaut (South Yemen today), who came to India in the nineteenth century. The Yemenis also served the nizam as military men. The plight of both the Yemenis and the Africans in Hyderabad, post-independence, is similar—they are ex-military personnel, who were discharged from service and retired, now living in barracks.

In the fifth century, when Sri Lanka was an emporium in the Indian Ocean, Abyssinians were trading in Mātota (a northwestern province). In the fourteenth century, when Ibn Batuta, the Moroccan traveler, visited the island, 500 Abyssinians were in the garrison of Jalasti, the ruler of Colombo. Marco Polo described Puttalama as "Battelar," the place that pearl fisheries used as a base for their operations in the Gulf. Batuta described it as "Battela" and a pretty little place surrounded by a timber wall and towers, which are generally associated with Puttalama (Ranasinha 1950:122). In addition, the Puttalama district is important to the Sinhalese who consider it to be the landing place of Vijaya, their ancestor (Ranasinha 1950:122).

According to the Afro-Sri Lankans who I interviewed, their ancestors were brought to Sri Lanka by the Europeans; this identifies their migration with Sri Lanka's colonial era that began in the sixteenth century and lasted until the middle of the twentieth century. Oral accounts are fragmented, but historical documents confirm that the successive waves of Portuguese, Dutch and British traders and colonizers brought Africans with them or imported them while they were in Sri Lanka (de Silva Jayasuriya 2003b).

Africans prolonged Portugal's dominance in Sri Lanka. In 1630, a Portuguese defeat in Sri Lanka was prevented by reinforcements of African soldiers sent from Goa who were paid salaries for their military services (de Silva Jayasuriya 1972). Sinhala literary works refer to the Africans in the Portuguese forces. The seventeenth-century war poem "Parangi Hatana" (War with the Portuguese) mentions the *Kāberis* (from the Portuguese word *cafre*, in turn borrowed from Arabic *qafr*), who were steeped in *kansa* and opium—and witless with drink. The Sinhala poem, "Rājasiha Hatana" (War with Rājasinghe), also refers to Kāberis. In 1586, according to the eye-witness account of Captain João Ribeiro, who served the Portuguese in Sri Lanka, the few Kaffirs who defected from the Portuguese fought for the Sinhalese army, serving Rājasinghe I of Sitawaka (1581–93), whose kingdom adjoined that of Kōtte (Pieris 1909). The king of the Kandyan kingdom befriended the Dutch in order to drive out the Portuguese from the island. When the Dutch defeated the Portuguese in 1658, some Africans who served the Portuguese joined the Kandyan king's army.

When the Dutch defeated the Portuguese in 1658, most Kaffirs simply changed masters. In 1694, for example, Colombo had 52.31% slaves who were from varied ethnic origins and different racial categories (Negroid, Mongoloid, and Caucasian). As Vink (2003:149) points out, slavery was a defining aspect of Dutch colonial settlements throughout the pre-existing open system of slavery in the commercialized and cosmopolitan cities in southeastern Asia and other parts of the Indian Ocean. The Dutch acquired most of their slaves through indigenous slave dealers. The officials of the *Vereenigde Oostindische Compagnie* (VOC) considered Africans more suitable for hard labor and thus they were generally field laborers who grew rice, *nacheri* (fine grain), cotton, tobacco, potatoes, and other crops. In Colombo, the Dutch maps marked the Kaffirs' *Veldt* (field) which is today's Echelon Square, near the Presidential Secretariat.

The largest community of Afro-Sri Lankans is now in the Puttalama district. In the 1970s, during a Sri Lankan television broadcast (Rupavāhini Corporation), the grand matriarch and leader of the Afro-Sri Lankan community, Ana Miseliya, revealed that her ancestors were brought by the "Europeans" to Trincomalee (eastern province) to assist in a war. The Africans had won the war for the Europeans and hoisted the flag in the Trincomalee fortress. Once the war was over, the Europeans took the Africans from Trincomalee along the Anuradhapura Road to Puttalama, so that they could be shipped back. However, the Africans refused to leave Sri Lanka—and the Sirambiyadiya inhabitants are the descendants of the Africans who remained. Afro-Sri Lankans can be found in many parts of the island, but the reason for the existing large community in the northwestern province is the disbanding of the African garrison within the Puttalama fortress in 1865. There are some Afro-Sri Lankans in other areas in the Puttalama district (Tabbova, Sellan Kandel, and Puttalama Town) and in other provinces as well (de Silva Jayasuriya 2007a).

Southeast Asia

Farther east in Asia, Africans were included in the census reports of Malaya and the colony of Singapore for the first half of the twentieth century. There were eighteen Africans in 1921, fourteen in 1931 and six in 1947. The 1881 population census of Malacca included Africans, but they were not numerous; the miscellaneous group, which included Achinese, Anamese, Bengalis, Bugis, Dyaks, Manilamen, Siamese, and Singhalese, totaled 174.

In Korea, Tim Bok Rae (2006) identifies an African who accompanied a Portuguese on the ship sailing from Nagasaki–it drifted to Korea but there is as yet no evidence of African settlers. She, however, draws attention to the indigenous Korean system of slavery, *Nobi*, which existed from very early times (Rae 2004).

In Timor, Africans were reported even in more recent times. The Portuguese troops in Timor included Africans. Around 1879, the Governor of Timor had a battalion which included 200 Africans (Pélissier 1996), who Hans Hagerdal (2007:personal communication) points out are called *Falikas*. Having carried out archival research on Timor, he has only come across one African servant in Timor in the seventeenth century. More archival research and fieldwork may reveal Timor's African connections. In Timor, there were 304 Africans in 1919; in 1927, 101 Africans; in 1930, only thirty; in 1936, 157; and in 1956, fifty-four Africans (Mendes Corea 1994:192). The larger variation in the numbers can be explained by the Portuguese moving their forces from one part of their empire to another.

It is often assumed that West Africans were taken across the Atlantic, while East Africans were traded across the Indian Ocean. Sometimes, this pattern was altered and West Africans also migrated to Asia. Although this may not appear to be geographically sensible, there are other reasons behind this unexpected occurrence. In Ghana, slaves bought their freedom on enlisting, using the advance payment for their services made by the Dutch. The Dutch were not engaged in slave trading in the Atlantic, due to this ingenious arrangement; they were simply recruiting Africans for their army who were entitled to equal treatment in terms of salary, food, and clothing, in theory, at least. Having paid off their debt to the Dutch in two or three years, initially, most Ghanaians opted to repatriate to Africa after their term of service was over. Yet from the mid-nineteenth century onwards, most veterans settled in Java. This change probably reflects acculturation of the Ghanaians to Indonesian society.

In the nineteenth century, 3,000 Ghanaians sailed to the East Indies to work for the Dutch colonial army. This migration continued from 1831 to 1872. After Abolition, the Dutch were unable to recruit slaves in the Atlantic. It was inconceivable that Ashantis, a proud people, would serve a foreign nation so the Dutch agents recruited those who had been enslaved by the Ashantis themselves. Mainly recruited from Kumas, these slaves were brought to Elmina on the Ghanaian coast and trained at the Fort Saint Jago. Then, they were taken to Jakarta, the capital of Indonesia. The Dutch had allowed them to return to Elmina once they retired from the army. Some of them remained with their Indonesian wives and families, but after 1955, they were forced to leave Indonesia with the Dutch and the Indo-Europeans.

Since the Dutch kept records of these movements and recent migrations—in comparison to other Indian Oceanic migrations—important clues as to how migrants adjusted to their new environments are available. While it is impossible to generalize about adjustment processes of the migrants due to the varying circumstances in their host societies, the Ghanaian soldiers nevertheless shed some light on what may have happened to other Africans who migrated to other Asian lands at earlier times.

For example, the Portuguese moved Africans as far as China and Japan. As a migrant labor force caught up in European commercial expansion, once the European domination ended, and when the Europeans withdrew from Asia, the Africans were generally marginalized in their new surroundings. As people in-between the colonizer and the colonized, and having been identified with the colonial powers, they generally have suffered after decolonization.

Friar Domingo Navarrete recorded the presence of black soldiers in Canton between 1618 and 1686. These "negroes" had been runaway slaves from Macau (Cummins 1962:138). Large numbers of African slaves lived in Macau and in 1640; there were "about 5,000" of them (Boxer, 1948:143, 223-236). Friar Domingo adds that on Sundays and Holy days the Parish Priest of Canton would say Mass for the wives of the "negroes" (Cummins 1962:232).

Peter Mundy also refers to the African servants of the Portuguese in Macau. Writing in October 1637 on Portuguese recreational habits, Mundy (1907:267) stated that the male slaves were "curled head Caphers [kafir, negro]," while the female slaves were Chinese.

Bodomo (2006) brought to my attention an emerging Afro-Chinese community in Hong Kong, namely the Tsim Sha Tsui's Chungking Mansions dwellers. As he points out, Hong Kong is a cosmopolitan city with diverse ethnic groups. As a kind of international emporium, it attracts various groups of migrants, particularly from less developed countries, who live in low cost accommodation in Chungking Mansions and guest rooms. They become part of an urban community of migrants driven by commercial activities. Judging by the languages that they speak, these new migrants originate from various ethnolinguistic groups. They are mother-tongue speakers of Twi, Igbo, Dagbami, Ewe, Ga, Kiswahili, Hausa, Kikuky, Kinande, Lingala, and Zulu. Using the case of Hong Kong's Chungking Mansions as an example, Bodomo draws attention to the emerging African communities in China's urban centers. In addition, Bodomo explores the demographic, sociolinguistic, and sociocultural profiles of this community. It would be of ethnomusicological value to ascertain what African musical traditions these communities have retained.

Boxer (1969:57) states that Portuguese shipping in the interport trade was increasingly operated by Asian seamen who worked under a few European and Eurasian officers. Even the great 1,000 to 2,000 ton carracks that sailed between Goa, Macau, and Nagasaki were manned by Asians and "Negro" slaves, except for the ship's officers and fifteen to twenty soldiers or gunners who were Europeans. Aminaka (2006:221) examines *nanban byoubu*—Japanese paintings—that depict Africans who came with the Portuguese; they show Africans dressed in western clothing and working with the Portuguese.

As more scholars embark on researching the diaspora in the East, the hitherto unknown Afro-Asian communities might come to light—all of which could likely interest the international academic community, welfare organizations and UN agencies who may have different agendas. A poem composed by Dr. Hemal Jayasuriya captures the underlying theme of this chapter.

Uprooted

Across the yawning sea
They came some
Of their own accord
Others against their will
Weaving a thread
Of a new tongue
On board their ships
Riding favourable monsoon winds
Bringing peoples to an eastern land
Where the sun set in the ocean
They togethered as one
Worked obediently for their masters
Surviving turbulent times
And found their feet in some calm after the storm.

CHAPTER 3

Dispersal of Africans across the Indian Ocean

Migration can involve movement over short or long distances within the same country or to another country. Sometimes migrating people even settle within their own cultural matrix. Financial, political, and sociological factors often force people to move from one place to another. An outcome of European exploration and western colonization was the sudden increase in long-distance migration, with the Indian Ocean becoming a site of multi-directional movement. Arabs and Indians had already been engaged in intra-Indian Oceanic trade—and African migration, both forced and voluntary, prevailed before Europeans even sailed the Indian Ocean.

The Indian Ocean was navigatable by use of the monsoon winds. From April to September, it was possible to sail from East Africa to Asia and then to return between November and February. Using the monsoons (trade winds), the dhows networked East Africa with Arabia, Persia, India, and other countries in the Indian Ocean world.

Pre-Western Interactions

Some Africans traveled over land while others were brought by sea. Given the lack of historical records among the migrants and the host countries, oral histories and traditions are crucial in unravelling and telling the stories of migrants and their arrival. Collins (2006:325) describes history as a member of the humanities family, not as a social science. According to him, history is the search for every available source, using any discipline to narrate a story. It is not bound by any rigid theoretical or methodological concepts. He adds that history describes what happened in the past—where, when, how, and why.

Involuntary African migration across the Indian Ocean coincided with the labor requirement and sociocultural values of the Arabs. Their mastery of the monsoons and domination of the Indian Ocean commerce enabled them not only to enslave Africans, who were then taken to the Middle East, but also to supply slaves to India (Pinto 2006:384). Most Africans who came to India were taken to Arabia first and then transported on to India's west coast—Kutch, Surat, and Bombay, for example.

After the seventh century, the Arab traders introduced Islam to people on the trade route. The *Hajj* (pilgrimage) route overlapped with the pattern of commerce, since it crossed from western Sudan, south of Lake Chad, to the Nilotic Sudan and the Red Sea ports (La Rue 2004:36).

The East African coast was a trading center for Arabian, Persian, Indian and Chinese merchants. Persians and Chinese followed the Arabs in intra-Asian trading. The Chinese traded with Africans during the Sung (1127–1279) and Ming (1368–1644) dynasties. In addition to ivory, rhino horn and tortoise shells, a few Africans were taken back to China. They were usually females, who became concubines (Collins 2006:337).

Braudel (1993:131) mentions that caravans brought about 18,000 to 20,000 slaves from Dar-Fur to Cairo in a single journey. In 1830, dues were being claimed for 37,000 slaves per annum by the Sultan of Zanzibar. In 1872, about ten or twenty thousand slaves had left Suakin for Arabia.

From the East African coast, slaves were shipped to the island of Socotra (now part of Yemen) and to Aden in Yemen. They were then taken to Egypt and Mesopotamia via the Red Sea and the Persian Gulf. Slaves were brought to Zanzibar, Kilwa, and Pemba by caravans from the interior. During the internal wars in Africa, slaves were captured in the center and taken to the coastal ports. It must be recognized that all enslaved Africans were not necessarily from the coast. The interaction between the hinterland and coast—and also between the islands, Socotra, Zanzibar and Mozambique Island, and the coast, should not be overlooked in the context of the slave trade and African migration.

Slaves from Ethiopia, Kenya, Somalia, Zanzibar, Kilwa, and other coastal regions in East Africa were sold to the Middle East and India before the Portuguese sailed the Indian Oceanic waters in the late fifteenth century. Since early medieval times, Africans came to India through Arabia, the Persian Gulf, and the Red Sea. They came to northwest Indian ports (Kutch, Gujarat), the western coast (Surat, Nasik, Bombay, Janjira Island, Goa), and the northeast (Kolkata – Calcutta).

The capital of Oman, Muscat, was the trans-shipment center on the Persian Gulf and India for African slaves to the Arab world. African slaves were also transported across the Red Sea, Tajura, Berbera, and Zanzibar to Asia. Enslaved Africans were taken on Arab dhows from East Africa to Oman from Ras Assir, which was known as "The Cape of Slaves," Zanzibar and Pemba Islands.

In 1840, Sayyid Said ibn Sultan, the ruler of Oman, transferred his court to Zanzibar, which had become the center of his empire by then—and the largest slave market in the East, the supplier of cloves to the world, and the main sales outlet for ivory. In 1856, when he died, Zanzibar became independent and was ruled by his son Majid. In 1859 alone, 19,000 slaves arrived in Zanzibar; most of them came from the Lake Nyasa area. They arrived in Kilwa and then two thirds were shipped to Zanzibar.

Ethiopians from Oromo (often called *Galla*, a derogatory term given to them by the Amhara) were apparently the most sought after slaves. The females were considered beautiful and the males were thought to be intelligent (Segal 2001:154). By the nineteenth century, Oromo slaves dominated the markets at Gondar and Gallabar in northwestern Ethiopia. Even Oromo chiefs supplied slaves to Muslim dealers. In 1866, many Christian Oromo were sold—as many as 500 a day in Gallabar alone. Muslim dealers collected slaves at Zeila and Tajurra and shipped them to Egypt, Arabia and Turkey (Segal 2001:154).

The Red Sea, whose main ports were under Ottoman rule, was the route that many slaves from East Africa took during the nineteenth century. By the 1860s, as many as 15,000 slaves per year were on Ottoman ships during the pilgrimage. These slaves were sold at Jedda and Mecca, or exchanged for goods such as steel weapons from Damascus, carpets or turquoise from Persia, and silks and jewelery from the Far East. Turkish pilgrims returning from Mecca and Medina brought African slaves back to Anatolia. In 1878, according to the *Anti-Slavery Reporter*, 25,000 slaves were sold or exchanged in Medina and Mecca every year. By 1884, an estimated number of 8,000 slaves per year were expected from Ethiopia, according to the London *Anti-Slavery Reporter*. In 1903, King Manelik decreed an end to the slave trade throughout Ethiopia; however, the trade continued.

Enslaved Africans were brought through ports in Gujarat, Bombay, Cambay, Cutch, and Mundra to India. Arabs and Gujaratis mediated in the slave trade. Machado (2004:27) draws attention to the Indian

A View of Mocha about 1830:
Arab Houses within the Walls and African Huts Outside
(Source: Robin Bidwell, *Travellers in Arabia*. Reading: Garnet, 1994)

involvement in the Mozambique-Portuguese India slave trade nexus through his study of the century from 1730 to 1830. Indian ships returning from Mozambique may have brought slaves to Mocha where they were sold to provide labor for coffee plantations (Machado 2004:19).

Arabs brought African slaves to India's west coast and Bengal in the Northeast. Since Arabs dominated the Indian Ocean from the sixth century, it is not surprising that they—and not the Portuguese—first introduced Africans to India. According to Banaji (1932:20), the Arabs were the main promoters of the African slave trade in India. Given India's large population and its own *dasas* (slaves), it seems doubtful that Indians would have actively sought African slaves. Outsiders may have been needed only to fill a gap in the labor market, especially if Indians themselves refused to perform certain jobs. However, the caste system in India generally takes care of this since different tasks are performed by specific groups called *jāti*.

If the Africans offered special skills that were in demand by the Indians, giving rise to a situation where Africans had a comparative advantage, then there would have been a demand for them. The Africans were important to the Indian elite, who were constantly under threat of invasions and had to defend their territories. Africans were good soldiers and their loyalty was equally valuable. Although they were "outsiders," they were generally loyal to their masters. Indians could not trust their own kith and kin, and those outside the kin system filled the gap in the defense sector.

By the eighth century, India had a significant slave market—and traded in African slaves from Ethiopia and East Africa (between Mozambique and Somalia). North of Mumbai, the port of Thane was an important entrepôt for African slaves and other goods. The majority of Africans came to India through Arabia and the Persian Gulf, entering through ports in the Sindh (today's Pakistan) and Gujarat.

Pinto (2006:384) points out that ancient India, both in the Vedic and Epic periods, had slaves, but that the hierarchical caste system and the feudalism of the Middle Ages culminated in "ugly" forms of human exploitation and bondage. Female slaves in India were also used as concubines and prostitutes. Chattopadhyay (1963:196) described slavery in

Assam before the British occupation in 1826, noting that sometimes even free men were relegated to slavery and given to the King's spiritual advisors, courtiers, and nobles. This practice of royal gifts, including slaves, to the temple for the needs of the religious institution was also followed by private benefactors—men with no children or relatives to whom to bequeath their slaves would earn merit by donating them as the slaves of God. Pandit Vishnu Datta Dalai, a Brahman Chief Priest of the temple of the Hindu Goddess, Durga said that the *Raja* (King) had assigned twelve villages to the temple of the Goddess and twenty-five slaves to the Goddess herself (Dalai 1839:29).

In Islamic countries where migrants have converted and assimilated, it is difficult to find African communities. However, in the Maldives, situated west of Sri Lanka, African descendants have remained isolated in particular islands. This offers an opportunity to explore important aspects of African contributions to contemporary Maldivian culture. Under Islam, slaves could earn their freedom. The price of freedom was fixed, and upon payment, the slaves earned their freedom. A freed male slave became a client of his former master, whose family name and lineage he had to adopt. Female slaves could be "objects" of enjoyment for their masters until they were given in marriage. A master had a moral obligation to marry off his slave. Better yet, a slave owner who educated his slave and then married her off would be rewarded in heaven.

Females were also needed for entertainment—to perform as musicians, singers and dancers. Schools in Baghdad, Cordoba, and Medina provided the necessary skills for these pursuits, and needless to say, these slaves commanded high prices. Other slaves were needed as domestic workers, cleaners and cooks, washerwomen, and nursemaids. Several were required as concubines and there was no social stigma attached to it. Once a concubine bore her master a child, she could not be sold or given away. Masters often married their concubines. Although wives could be divorced, such concubines stayed permanently with their master.

The slave route illustrates the spatial movement of enforced African migration. African homelands (coastal and hinterland), markets, and ports in Africa and Asia became important as market places where human beings could be bought and sold. The slave route also shows economic activity—and reflects the deployment of military and administrative resources of colonial powers. The routes taken by the slaves marked the trail of trading patterns, showing the economic power bases of Asia. The economic importance of slavery was tied to the paths on which slaves were taken. Slaves added value to the commercial operations of colonizers. Since they were costless or lowly paid workers, they enhanced the profit margins by enormous amounts. Slaves built fortresses for the Europeans in Asia and worked in the fields as well. Some of them worked as house slaves and the females often became concubines. The slave route shows the pattern of movement; it shows the vital role that Africans played in the maritime activities in the East. It also reveals where economic power—indigenous as well as imperial—lay.

It is also noteworthy that Cape Town does not feature as a point from which Africans were transported to the East. The aggression of the southern African tribes such as Zulus made it difficult to capture them. The undesirability of Hottentots, who were not considered physically strong enough, may have been another reason for this exclusion. Even if the Portuguese ships were adequately manned, by the time they reached the Cape, they would have required more manpower as they expended resources and men while they sailed to eastern Africa. Ironically, Cape Town received many Asian slaves from the Dutch East Indies, mainly from Batavia (today's Jakarta). Between 1658 and 1807, more than 60,000 slaves (Asian, Malagasy, and East African) lived in the Cape. These slaves, together with South African born slaves and unfree Khoi and San laborers, equaled or outnumbered the European settlers and officials during the eighteenth century and the early decades of the nineteenth century (Worden 2007:10). This is significant because the Dutch were masters of the Indian Ocean in the seventeenth century and were responsible for moving Asians to Africa.

Portuguese Intervention into Asian Maritime Trade

Building empires in far flung domains required manpower. Therefore, it is not surprising that commercial ventures—Dutch East India Company

(VOC) and the English East India Company (EIC)—indulged in the slave trade. The Portuguese *Estado da India* was no exception. African migration across the Indian Ocean was stimulated by European entry into Asian waters for trading activities. Africans had migrated eastward before the Portuguese domination of Indian Oceanic trade in the sixteenth century, which nevertheless led to further displacements of Africans to the East (de Silva Jayasuriya 2006b). The Portuguese ushered the Dutch, French, and British into the Asian trade networks—and this led to further movements of Africans across the Indian Ocean.

The Portuguese were confronted with a complex economic system when they first sailed the Indian Ocean. They had already made contact with West Africa and owned African slaves as fieldworkers and house slaves. This influenced their attitude towards Africans. Building a maritime empire resulted in unusual demands, not least on the social world and communication on board the ship. Managing a maritime empire that stretched across three continents was no simple task.

Until the twelfth century, Portugal was part of the Islamic kingdom of Al-Andalus in the Iberian Peninsula. The new nation was born in 1139, when Afonso I. Henriques became the first King of Portugal. Due to the mountainous nature of Portugal and its restricted agricultural economy, most Portuguese settled on the coast which gave them an advantage in seafaring. After the capture of Cueta in 1415, Portuguese exploration of West Africa increased.

Saunders (1982:33) points out that after the 1440s, when slaves were captured through the warlike raids on the Mauritanian coast, the Portuguese liaised with African princes and merchants to find slaves. The Portuguese had a royal monopoly on western African trade which meant that private traders had to obtain a licence to trade there. The Portuguese established the *Casa dos Escravos* (house of slaves) in Lisbon to regulate and draw fiscal benefits from slave trading. Saunders (1982:33) estimates that during 1510 and 1550, for example, up to 3,500 Africans per year were enslaved from Upper Guinea, and that at least 2,000 were taken from the Kongo and Angola. All these Africans did not go to Portugal and many were resold to Spain and the Spanish colonies in the Americas. After 1535, Spanish demand for slaves increased, probably after the conquest of Peru. This foreign demand for slaves not only drove up the price of slaves in Lisbon, but it also meant that new sources of supply had to be found. The Portuguese conquest of Angola, farther down on the African coast, resulted from this increased demand. Between 1511 and 1559, Portuguese quintupled their profits from West African trade (Saunders 1982:34). Slaves were one of the main commodities in this lucrative trade. The Portuguese counted the *cabeças de pessoas* ("heads of people") whose value was measured in terms of cowrie shells.

During the fifteenth century, Africans were already in Portugal, working as household slaves and in farms. Some of these Africans had been captured during slave raids. Saunders (1982:5–7) reports that two Portuguese vessels docked at the Rio de Oro and carried off several local Berbers including one of Idzāgen's "black" slave women. The captives served as useful informants to the Portuguese. Two years later, a Portuguese *caravel* returned to ransom a pair of aristocratic Idzāgen in exchange for ten black slaves and some gold. In 1445, Gomes Pires exchanged "black" slaves for trade goods. After 1448, the Portuguese made contact with black princes who had many prisoners of war and criminals for sale. Portuguese trade with the Idzāgen was conducted at Arguim, an island off the Mauritanian Coast. South of Senegal, the trade was conducted from ship to shore. The Portuguese king and his ministers created a black slave community in Portugal.

In 1466, the island of Santiago and Cape Verde Islands became bases for Portuguese trade with Upper Guinea. In 1471, the Portuguese "discovered" the "Mine," the Gold Coast, so called because the Africans brought gold from the hinterland to that part of the shore for trading purposes. When the fort São Jorge da Mina was constructed in 1482, slaves acquired farther east, along the West African coast in Benin and the Slave Rivers, were bartered for gold. These activities continued until the 1530s when the Portuguese King, João III, declared that it was immoral for Christians to sell slaves to infidels. In 1493, São Tome became a clearing house for slaves acquired in Benin and the Congo. The Portuguese penetrated the Congo in 1483 and evangelization began in 1490. However, within a few decades, the slave trade superseded evangelization as the main Portuguese interest in the Congo. The number of Africans,

mostly enslaved and some freed, in Lisbon was significant during the fifteenth and sixteenth centuries. In Portugal, many Africans and other
slaves performed tasks that were considered undesirable by the
Portuguese. It therefore follows that Africans performed menial tasks on
the voyages, in addition to being sailors. Slaves manned the ships plying
between Lisbon and Africa and were also on board smaller vessels that
sailed the rivers and along the coasts of Portugal. In addition, Portuguese
seamen were able to persuade their employer to hire their slaves so that
they could work side by side (Saunders 1982:75). Through this arrangement, the owner of the slave benefited from the wages paid to his slave.

Given the significant African presence in Lisbon during the fifteenth
century, ships sailing to India from Lisbon would have included Africans
on board. Depending on the route of the particular voyage, the number
would have been augmented by Africans taken on board from El Mina
(Ghana), Mouth of the River Congo, Niger Delta, Sierra Leone, the
Azores, Canary Islands, Madeira, Mozambique, and Madagascar. By the
time the Portuguese reached India by sea, in the late fifteenth century,
Abyssinians were already in India.

In 1634, Bocarro (1634:14), the Portuguese chronicler, reported that
married Portuguese owned some 2,000 slaves of various races. In 1653,
Bocarro recorded that out of the 500 homes in the Portuguese city of
Nagapatnam, South India, 140 were occupied by "white" Portuguese and
the *mulattos* (the offspring of Portuguese and Africans), and "native"
Christians with Indian slaves lived in the other houses (Schurhammer
1977:549).

In the first quarter of the sixteenth century, when Portugal was mak-
ing initial contact with many Asian countries, the population of
Portugal was about one-and-a-half million. The Portuguese voyages of
discovery began a commercial revolution. Portugal's foray into the
Indian Ocean, which led to establishing a maritime trade route to the
East, stimulated the slave trade. The long and treacherous voyage to
India cost many lives. Portugal had been thinly populated and the slave
trade provided an opportunity to obtain additional manpower. However,
Portuguese involvement in the African slave trade began even before the
Age of Discoveries.

From the days of Portuguese exploration, slaves had been named *uma peça d'India,* meaning "a piece of India," as Africans were exchanged for Indian fabrics. Pedro Machado (2004:18) argues that slaves had become an important part of the commercial activities and revenue of Gujarati Indians in East Africa. The Portuguese competed with the Swahili Muslims and Indians for slaves on the African Coast. The events in Mozambique and Mozambique Island illustrate the demand for slaves by competing groups—Arabs, Swahili, Indians, and Portuguese. As a result, the Portuguese curbed the trade of all non-Christians. The Indians had reacted by petitioning and argued that they, as Hindus, were not converting the Africans. Moreover, they pointed out that they only accepted slaves in return for Gujarati cloth because there were no other "satisfactory goods" in Africa (Machado 2004:18). They assured the Portuguese that the slaves would be sold to the Portuguese when they left Mozambique. They even allowed the Portuguese to convert their slaves to Catholicism and encouraged the converted slaves to attend church. By this time, slaves had become vital commodities to Indian merchants in Mozambique—and they threatened to leave Mozambique if the Portuguese banned them from owning slaves. These slaves serviced the houses and met other requirements of the Indians. In 1746, the Portuguese granted the Indians permission to own and trade in slaves, recognizing the vital economic role they played in Mozambique at that time. A few Indians owned more than ten slaves, but most of them owned about two or three slaves (Machado 2004:19).

In India, the Christian clergy and the nobility employed African slaves. Daman and Diu, both located in today's State of Gujarat, were among Portugal's last holdings in India. They fell back into Indian hands in 1961, along with Goa. In 1660, it was estimated that there were about 600 Africans in Daman Praça. The Captain Governor of Daman alone had thirty or forty African servants (Moniz 1923:156). In the Goa archives, historical records reveal that in 1792, 598 slaves lived in Diu (Pinto 2006:388). African slaves arrived in Daman as late as 1828. In 1838, 6% of Diu's population was African (Carreira 1998:686).

John Huyghen Van Linschoten (1885:275–276), the sixteenth-century Dutch traveler, recorded that:

From Mozambique great numbers of these Caffares are carried into India, and many times they sell a man or woman that is growne to their full [strength], for two or three Ducats. When the Portingales ships put in there for fresh water and [other] necessaries, then they are dearer, by reason of the great numbers of buyers, the cause why so many slaves and Captaines of all nations are brought to sell in India, is, because that everie ten or twelve miles, or rather in every Village and towne, there is a severall King, and ruler of the people, one of them not like an other, neither in law, speech, nor manners, whereby most part of them are in warres, one against the other, and those that on both sides are taken [prisoners] they kéepe or slaves, and so sell each other like beastes: hee whose evill fortunely is such that hee is one of the captives, must be patient wherein they shew not much dislike, for when they are asked, how they can content themselves [with that yoke of bondage], they answere that they can beare it well [enough], seeing their Planet will have it so, and for that their friends and neighbors shall revenge their cause against those that have done it. Also in time of povertie or dearth the fathers may sell their children, ... and because the Portingales have traffique in all places (as we have beene in many) it is the cause why so many are brought out of all countries to be solde, for the Portingales does make a living by buying and selling [of them] as they doe with other wares. What concerneth the Caffares in Mozambique, I have in another place declared, in the description of Mozambique.

This account shows how the demand for slaves increased with the Portuguese entry onto the Indian Ocean. It also describes to some extent the indigenous system of slavery that existed and would have continued in India regardless of European intervention in Eastern commerce and colonization. More importantly, Linschoten describes the turmoil in India, which was troubled by wars between many kings. Defending one's kingdom was a real problem for an Indian king—and in my opinion, this was a catalyst for acquiring Africans for the sub-continent.

As a maritime state, Goa, the center of the *Estado da India*, was the location of several slaves and understandably, a slave market existed there. In addition to its position as the headquarters of the Estado da India, Goa became a supplier of African slaves to Portugal's other possessions in the East. This scenario peaked in the seventeenth century, but continued until the nineteenth century (Dos Martinez Lopes 1996:93; Bauss 1997:21).

The Marquis of Pombal found it offensive that Africans born in Portugal were disadvantaged. He was also apprehensive about the discriminatory distinctions made between old and new Christians. Therefore, in 1768, he abolished the distinction between the two categories of Christians. From 16 January 1773, he began to emancipate slaves, freeing them and removing legal constraints on children born after the date that their parents, grandparents, and great-grandparents had been slaves. Prior to this, in 1761, the import of slaves to Portugal had been banned—this was probably to reduce the slave population in the colonies. Slavery was outlawed in the Portuguese empire in 1875 (Saunders 1982:178). However, in 1815, Portugal abolished slave trading north of the equator and restricted exports to its possessions. Fifteen years later, in 1830, Portugal took measures to extend this legal restriction to the south of the equator. Portugal finally passed a decree forbidding participation in the slave trade and slavery in 1836. The Marquis of Sá da Bandeira was the force behind these turn of events. After three decades of *portarias* (parliamentary decrees), slavery itself was banned in 1869. In 1875, the Portuguese Empire outlawed slavery in all its colonies. However, in Brazil, one of Portugal's colonies, slavery was abolished as late as 1888.

When David Livingstone, the British medical missionary, visited the Mbari ethnic group in 1851, which inhabits today's Central Africa, the Africans were exchanging slaves for Manchester cotton goods (Willis 2003:5). *Pombeiros* (Afro-Portuguese) were bartering muskets for slaves at that time.

In East Africa, Livingstone found three groups of slave dealers: *prazeiros* (land grant holders), pombeiros, and the Arab and Swahili traders of the sultan of Zanzibar. Africans often sold themselves to the prazeiros. According to Clive Willis (2003:18), by an odd hierarchical ladder, these slaves had the opportunity to become richer than their masters, own slaves, and have families. The pombeiros abandoned trading in ivory and gold—and switched over to slave trading which was more profitable at that time. They also encouraged tribal chiefs to enslave their people so that the market would have an adequate supply of slaves.

Nevertheless, the Arab and Swahili traders were the most numerous of the three groups. They descended into the Lake Malawi region and traveled down the Shire River area capturing Africans. These captives were sent to the African coast from where they were shipped to islands in the Indian Ocean. These operations were curtailed by the British navy that patroled and looked out for ships carrying slaves on board.

Dutch Naval Power

The Portuguese, who entered the Indian Ocean at the turn of the fifteenth century, dominated the intra-Asian trade throughout the next century; however, they were soon outdone by Dutch commercial activity of the United East India Company, VOC (*Verenegde Oost-Indische Compagnie*). The VOC which received its Charter on 20 March 1602, had been endowed with powers to regulate and protect the eastern trade which they monopolized. The company was authorized to keep armed forces and to exercise administrative, judicial and legislative authority over the Eastern lands. There was a complex relationship between the governing body of the VOC which was in the Netherlands, its headquarters in Batavia (called Jakarta today), and the colonies. The Dutch had a corporate proto-global identity. They had larger ships and were a stronger naval power than the Portuguese.

Even so, manning a geographically spread-out enterprise placed demands on Dutch human resources. Some of these deficiencies were filled by forced migrations of people from one colony to another. Asians—and not only Africans—fell victim to the slave trade and were displaced across the Indian Ocean. Some have mistakenly assumed that the Dutch enslaved Asians only. Clearly, this is not the case. In addition to the ingenious method used in nineteenth-century Ghana by the

Dutch to obtain soldiers without enslaving them, there were other examples of Dutch having African slaves.

The VOC monopolized the Indian Ocean trade. Barendse (1998:140) states that the Portuguese traders from Angoche would sometimes buy slaves from Madagascar and sell them in Muscat. In 1626, the VOC sent a ship to Madagascar so that slaves could be obtained for Batavia. But this was unsuccessful as many slaves died during the long voyage. It was more economical for the Dutch to buy slaves from India—Bengal and the Coromandel Coast—for their needs in Batavia, due to the geographical proximity.

Some slaves were obtained by wild slaving, burning down villages, and enslaving one's own people. For example, between 1640 and 1644, the Dutch in Mauritius shipped excess slaves from Madagascar to Batavia. This was uneconomical but illustrates how difficult it was to control the stock of slaves. During the second half of the seventeenth century, the establishment of plantations in the southwest Indian Ocean islands—Mauritius, Bourbon, and St. Helena—was labor intensive, and thus stimulated the slave trade. The Dutch, French, and British obtained African slaves to meet their needs.

The VOC considered Mozambique and the Swahili coast remote and inadequately surveyed. Therefore, they turned to Madagascar for gold, ebony, and slaves (Barendse 1998:142). Malagasy slaves were strong, robust, and sturdily built—and so they could be used for heavy work. At the beginning of the eighteenth century, slaves were bought by the VOC for Sri Lanka as well (Pieters 1911:21). Malagasy slaves, obtained through Bourbon, were also transported to Batavia (today's Jakarta) in Indonesia and to Pondicherry in India. They labored as construction workers or as henchmen of the bailiff ("bullies") (de Haan 1922, 1935:145–172). The Dutch authorities in Batavia were ambivalent about Malagasy slaves who were often less likely to run away because they were not familiar with Indonesia. Yet, they failed to live up to Dutch expectations and were not generally used as house slaves. Balinese slaves were domestics in Batavia. This kind of functional specialization of slaves might not have racial undercurrents and simply suggests that the Dutch liked to work with the established system as much as possible when feasible.

Malagasies were chattel slaves of the VOC in Batavia; they were not sold to individuals. Therefore, in Batavia and Bencoolen, Malagasies formed distinct communities and lived in separate barracks. While freed Asian slaves from Bali and Sulawesi flourished in Batavia, the fate of Malagasies was different. The distinction between a house slave and chattel slave appears to have had repercussions on the Malagasies, understandably; the death rate among Malagasies was high. For the Malagasies, the process of adjustment would have been demanding. Long-distance migration and dislocation would have taken a toll on them. The VOC administrators in Batavia ordered that young slaves, aged between sixteen and twenty-four only, should be purchased, as they believed that the older Malagasies would be more homesick, pine for Madagascar, and not survive in the new environment.

The Dutch in Sri Lanka consisted of the VOC employees and the *Vrijburgers* ("free burghers"). The distinction between these two categories was not maintained in the British era (1796–1948) and both groups became known as *Burghers*. The Vrijburgers came to Sri Lanka for private business (bakeries, inns, and taverns, for example) and trade. From the time Colombo was captured by the Dutch in 1656, it became the seat of government. Its inhabitants were mainly Sinhalese Buddhists. The Vrijburgers engaged slaves as artisans or laborers in their businesses. When the British took over, the Burghers, who consisted of both the VOC officials and the Vrijburgers, were reduced to a lower socioeconomic status—and their slaves also suffered as a consequence. Nevertheless, slaves were income-generating assets and were hired out by their owners whenever they needed extra income. This practice was known among the Portuguese and the Muslims. In West Africa, Muslims allowed their slaves to work so that they could provide an income for their master (Lovejoy 2004b:244). This practice, known as *murgu*, also gave slaves an opportunity to accumulate enough money to buy their freedom.

According to the Dutch Governor, Van Goens Junior (who served in Sri Lanka from 1675–80), 4,000 Kaffirs were engaged in building the fortress in Colombo at the beginning of Dutch rule in the Maritime Provinces. Colombo was seriously ravaged and depopulated because of the battles between the Portuguese and Dutch. The VOC had to import foodstuffs, as Colombo could not be supplied with food from its hinterland at that time. From 1681 onwards, however, economic ties with the hinterlands were restored and the Sinhalese came to Colombo to sell their produce (rice, cattle, and other foodstuffs) in the market. The VOC largely monopolized the foreign trade of Colombo, exporting cinnamon and betel nuts and importing textiles, provisions, building materials, and slaves. The VOC built a *kasteel* (castle) which is known as the *Fort* in modern Colombo. The old walls and bulwarks of the eastern part of Portuguese Colombo were preserved as a safe haven for the indigenous population during times of danger, in an area which was known as the *stad* (town) which is a busy commercial location called Pettah today.

According to Emerson Tennent, Colonial Secretary of Ceylon (1845–1849), the Dutch kept up the number of Kaffirs by immigration from the Cape. Almost a century later, Elsie Cook, an educational advisor to the British Colonial Office, who inspected the Buddhist English schools and the two Buddhist training schools for teachers in Sri Lanka, stated that "the European custom of supplementing armies with foreign troops is also responsible for a slight *Kaffir* element in the population of Ceylon" (Cook 1953:272).

It is often assumed that Africans from the east coast migrated eastward and that those from the west coast crossed the Atlantic. Sometimes, this general trend was altered. The East India Company (VOC) possessed monopoly rights from the Cape of Good Hope to the East Indies which included India, Sri Lanka, and Malacca. The Dutch West Indian Company (WIC) and the Africa Company both were unhappy that slaves were sought from West Africa by the Dutch East India Company and the English East India Company because of their monopolies on other trade routes. The WIC was involved in the transatlantic triangular trade, taking slaves from West Africa across to the West Indies, Surinam, and Brazil, and then bringing goods back to the Netherlands. As a result, the United East India Company could not purchase slaves on Africa's west coast. However, Ghanaians were recruited for the Dutch colonial army to serve in Indonesia. Of course, this was not an indulgence in the slave trade, as the Dutch avoided problems by freeing them before they were enlisted. The Dutch government had to defend their recruitment of Africans, since the British accused the Dutch of slave trading covertly (Van Kessel 2002:134). In 1837, after the British and Dutch had abolished the slave trade, recruitment had to be voluntary— and an advance payment was given so that the slaves could purchase their freedom. At Elmina, the ex-slaves received a certificate of manu-mission which legally endorsed their status as free men (Van Kessel 2002:136).

In 1803, the slave trade was abolished in the Netherlands. Eleven years later, in 1814, the Dutch declared illegal the slave trade that orig-inated in its ports. The Dutch involvement in the slave trade was appar-ent during their seventeenth-century supremacy in the Asian waters. Arthur Burnell, who served in the Madras Civil Service, stated that the Dutch also imported African slaves to South India; he searched for their descendants in all the Portuguese and Dutch colonies, but was unable to locate any at that time (Linschoten 1885:33).

The Dutch domination of the maritime provinces of Sri Lanka includ-ed the suzerainty of the Maldives. Large quantities of cowries from the Maldives were exported via Sri Lanka to the European markets, espe-cially in Amsterdam. Cowries were the monetary units used to then pur-chase Africans from the Guinea Coast. The slave trade drove up the value and price of cowries. An anonymous Dutchman's records in the mid-eighteenth century, which was translated into English, provide a detailed account of the cowrie shells and the slave trade (Gray 1887:239):

> The Dutch drive a considerable trade with the inhabitants of the Maldives for these little shells called cowries, there are prodigious quantities of them, and not only on the shore, but in the very ground, being probably deposited there at the time of the Flood, and left there when the ocean receded from the land. What we call money being arbitrary, and its nature and value depending on a tacit convention betwixt men, these shells in several parts of Asia and Africa, were accounted current money, with a value assigned to them....

But their great currency is on the coast of Africa, particularly Guinea, where the negroes value them as much as gold and silver, and call them *bougies* [Portuguese *busios*)....

Formerly twelve thousand-weight of these cowries would purchase a cargo of five or six hundred negroes; but those lucrative times are now no more; and the negroes now set such a value on their countrymen, that there is no such thing as having a cargo under twelve or fourteen tons of cowries.

As payments in this kind of species are attended with some intricacy the negroes, though so simple as to sell one another for shells, have contrived a kind of copper vessel, holding exactly a hundred and eight pounds, which is a great dispatch to business.... The chief European market for these shells is Amsterdam, where there are spacious warehouses of them, the French and English merchants buying them up to send to Africa.

The French

French activities in the Indian Ocean and enclaves in India, Southeast Asia (Cambodia, Vietnam, and Laos), and the islands in the Southwest Indian Ocean involved shipping Africans to and fro—in both directions—across the Indian Ocean. Africans from Kilwa were taken to work on sugar and coffee plantations in the Mascarenes. French activities were mostly limited to the southwestern Indian Ocean islands. Some African slaves imported to Diu were then trans-shipped to India's French possession—Pondicherry and the Mascarenes as well. This may have been done via the Goan market, a seemingly illogical, circuitous route but commercially viable nonetheless.

Some uninhabited islands—Mauritius, Réunion, Seychelles, Rodrigues, and the Chagos—became populated during the European struggle for hegemony over the Indian Ocean region and trade monopolies in the East. European colonization brought together slaves and indentured laborers from Africa and Asia to work on plantations.

Houbert (2003) argues that these particular Indian Ocean islands have more in common with the far off islands in the West Indies than with their non-creole neighbors in the Indian Ocean world. On these islands, Newitt (2003) states, a second Caribbean was created in the Indian Ocean. The demand for slaves grew with the tobacco and sugar industry. Along with Rodrigues and Réunion, Mauritius forms part of the Mascarenes group of islands, which were named after the Portuguese explorer, Mascarenhas, who first charted the area in 1514. After two attempts, the Dutch abandoned their plans to colonize Mauritius. Two maroons, who survived the Dutch invasion in 1710, were the first settlers of Mauritius. The French occupied Mauritius from 1715 to 1810. Moutou (1985) estimates that out of a total population of about one million, 200,000 Mauritians could claim African roots.

The identity of the people of Mascarenes and Madagascar is ambiguous; they are part of the Indian Ocean and Asian in some cultural aspects, yet geographically and politically, they remain African. Since this book focuses on Africans who migrated to Asia, this particular inter-African migration will not be considered.

France abolished the slave trade three times. As early as 1794, the French revolutionary government prohibited slavery and the slave trade. Driven by the requirement for a labor supply to man the colonies, Napoleon reinstated the French slave trade and slavery in 1802. Thirteen years later, in 1815, France abolished the slave trade again. Then, in 1840, it abolished slavery and yet again in 1848.

The French controlled Trincomalee for a few months, but were unable to obtain more than a toehold in Sri Lanka. Yet, Joseph Fernando, who epitomized the military powers of Africans, was brought to Sri Lanka by a Monsieur Bellicombe, a French seaman/trader from Mauritius. Fernando fought off one of two unsuccessful British invasions of the Kandyan kingdom, which had remained independent throughout Portuguese and Dutch presence. Fernando was interviewed on 8 April 1848 when he was in his eighties and a pensioner. The interview alternates between Indo-Portuguese of Ceylon (Sri Lankan Portuguese Creole), the lingua franca, and Sinhala, the language of interethnic communication, with Fernando slipping back into Sinhala when he recollects the ruthless massacre of Major Davie, the leader of the British troops. This event took place in 1803, and the Sri Lankans were able to retain control of the Kandyan kingdom (de Silva Jayasuriya 2001a). During this war, eighty Kaffirs serving the Sri Lankan king defended the Kandyan kingdom and delayed its takeover until 1815 (Powell 1973).

By the mid-eighteenth century, enslaved Africans could be found in the French territories on the Coromandel coast (Catlin-Jairazbhoy and Alpers 2004:13). At present, little is known about them, but French archival sources may reveal more details. Several thousands of "indentured" East Africans, who were recruited to work in the cane fields of Réunion as late as the mid-nineteenth century, are considerd to be the manifestations of the slave trade in disguise (Pineo 1979; Gerbeau 1986:220-23, 236).

Growth of British Imperial Power

British participation in the Indian Ocean slave trade overlapped with their rising imperial power. Although heated debates on abolition were taking place in Britain, the British Parliament's 1807 Act did not stop the British from continuing to indulge in the slave trade.

According to the historian, Thomas (1997:570-571):

> Continuing English involvement in the trade is more difficult to analyse. A few dealers established in West Africa ... continued to play a part. Some English captains sailed under United States flags, and later under Swedish, Danish, and even French ones. More important, probably, several prominent firms participated in the trade after 1807 by investing in or even owning theoretically Spanish—or Portuguese—owned ships ... Many English firms still supplied the 'trade goods' for slave voyages.

By 1700, Britain's East India Company had many settlements, including those in India such as in Bombay and Calcutta. The British divided India into three Presidencies—Bombay, Calcutta, and Madras—for administrative convenience. Due to its proximity to Africa, Arabia and the Red Sea, the western coast of India became a site for imported Africans. As Banaji (1932) points out, official documents of the Bombay Presidency reveal that slaves were imported in Arab vessels to the states of Kutch, Kathiawar, Porbandar, Sindh, and Bombay, and to ports held by the Portuguese at that time as well in Goa, Daman, and Diu. These slaves had been distributed all over the Bombay Presidency.

In the Calcutta Presidency, Africans, called *Coffrees*, were advertised for sale. Pinto (2006:392) conjectures that in the Madras Presidency the Africans would be insignificant because of its praedial slavery, adding that in Madras, bonded slaves were available and therefore there was no need to import Africans. Nevertheless, she infers that the Portuguese would have brought a few Africans to the fisheries coast.

In 1851, Sir Richard Burton, who served in the British Army in the Sindh (a province in today's Pakistan), noted that six to seven hundred *Zangibari, Bambasi,* Habshi, and other "blacks" were imported annually from Africa to Baluchistan—and they cost anything from forty to 100 rupees. The girls were more in demand and therefore more expensive than boys. Habshi females were priced at around forty to fifty pounds. Child slaves were bartered for goods—mainly, grain and cloth. Many of them had been forcefully captured and sold at the Swahili coast. According to Beachey (1976:50), during the same period, male and female slaves were part of Baluchistan households. Omani Arabs were controlling the slave trade during this period from Zanzibar, with Gujarati Indians and Europeans trading in the slave market. Gujarati and Bania Indians in Zanzibar and Pemba owned about 6,000 Africans, both males and females (Beachey 1976:56). African servants became necessities in households of Indian government officials, landowners, merchants, and traders, who were anxious to flaunt their wealth and status.

Most of these slaves had come from the towns of Lamo, Baromaki, and Kinkwhere in the Kotomondo district, which adjoined the *Sawahil* (the Arabic word for "coasts") country. The slaves mentioned people in their original countries as being mainly Muslims and spoke about their forts, chiefs, and armies.

Phasing Out the Slave Trade and Slavery

According to Campbell (2004:ix), the slave trade in the Indian Ocean World is about 4,000 years old. In India, slavery existed among the Hindus. There were many ways by which people became slaves. The *Nānava-dharmaçastra* (viii, 15) mentions "the captive, a slave for keep, (a slave) born in the house, (one) bought or given, an ancestral (slave), a slave by punishment—those seven (are) slaves." According to Jolly (1876), the Institute of Nārada (v, 23-26) mentions:

> ... slaves, whereof there are fifteen kinds: 24. One born in the house; one bought; one received by donation; one got by inheritance; one maintained in a famine; one pledged by a former master. 25. One relieved from a great debt; one made prisoner in a war; one obtained through a wager; one who has offered himself, saying, "I am thine", an apostate from religious mendicity, a slave for a fixed period. 26. One maintained in reward of the work performed by him, a slave for the sake of his wife; and one self-sold, are the fifteen kinds of slaves declared by law.... 29. One maintained in a famine is released from slavery on giving a pair of oxen; for what has been consumed in a famine is not discharged by labour alone.

The attitudes of slave owners were not influenced by Buddhism, Hinduism, and Christanity (Campbell et al 2007:1). In contrast, a Muslim slave owner was governed by religious beliefs. His children from a slave mother were emancipated. Upon his death, the slave woman (the mother of his children) was also freed. Unlike Buddhists and Hindus, Christians and Muslims made conversions.

The Portuguese Crown's official propagandists had declared that West African blacks and Idzāgen were primitive peoples and enslaving and bringing them to Portugal would benefit them since they were converted to Christianity and introduced to European civilization (Saunders 1982:35). From the mid-sixteenth century, moral theologians opposed the Portuguese Crown's attitude to slavery, but this was not sufficient to stop slavery. This could be considered the first act that called for abolition, although Portugal passed a law to abolish the slave trade quite late.

In Sri Lanka, commenting on the Dutch practices that encouraged conversion to Calvinism, Bertolacci (1817), who served the British government in Sri Lanka from 1800–1816 and who held several offices including that of Comptroller-General of Customs and Acting Auditor-General of Civil Accounts, states that if slaves were married in the Dutch church (for which they required their master's consent), their children were freed; they were also freed after the death of their master and his wife. Married slaves could not be sold. The master had to comply with the Adoption Act, in which he was considered the guardian of the christened slave.

Slavery was abolished by eliminating its legal status, regardless of which European power was involved. Although there was much publicity surrounding the commemoration of the British Parliamentary Abolition of the Slave Trade Act of 1807, which made it illegal for African men, women, and children to be enslaved, Britain was not the first nation to pass such an act. In 1792, the Danish government declared that from 1803 it would be illegal to import slaves into its Caribbean islands. According to historian Eltis (1979:211):

> The flow of British resources into the slave trade did not cease in 1807. After this date British subjects owned, managed and manned slaving adventures; they purchased newly imported Africans in the Americas; they supplied ships, equipment, insurance, and most important of all trade goods and credit to foreign slave traders.

Sherwood (2007:3) points out that the British merchants, shipbuilders, insurers, bankers, manufacturers, and many workers and investors all profited from the slave trade and the use of slaves in plantations, farms, and mines until the final abolition of slavery by 1880 in Cuba, and by 1888, in Brazil.

In the context of involuntary African migration to Asia, some attention to the systems of slavery that existed, both in Africa and Asia, is needed. Africans were captured in internal wars and served their captors, with unpaid labor, for a limited time. When the Europeans began to sail down the African coast, Africans bartered their captives, their fellow-men, for goods, particularly guns, gunpowder, and rum. This exchange of "commodities" and external demand for African slaves created an increased demand which could not be met from the coast alone. Understandably, this resulted in slave raids during which Africans were kidnapped and captured from the hinterland; they were then brought to the coast and sold to Europeans.

Bertolacci (1817), who served the first British Governor of Sri Lanka, Sir Frederick North (1798–1805), commented on the stability of slavery in the transition period from Dutch to British rule in Sri Lanka. Surprisingly, in spite of the anti-slavery campaign and heightened public awareness, at least in Britain, Bertolacci predicted that British institutions would maintain the status quo. He felt that slavery would be perpetuated by the British laws instituted in Sri Lanka. As the major slave owners, the Burghers were reduced to a lower economic status, and Bertolacci predicted that their slaves would undergo an even harder life. He suggested that slavery could be abolished by either granting slave owners compensation or setting a date in the future, say in sixty or eighty years, when slavery would be abolished. The cost of the first option would fall on the British government. The second option would gradually decrease the value of slaves and would not cause grievance to slave owners.

The question of redeeming or transferring slaves arose when the British encountered the institution of slavery in Sri Lanka. The Commander of the British Expeditionary Force extended the meaning of "property" to include slaves. All slaves had to be registered. The slaves were restored to their owners. The British offered a sum of money for the maintenance of the slaves. Given the low profile of abolition in the Indian Ocean, close consideration of the Sri Lankan case is worthwhile. From the beginning of the nineteenth century, the British attempted to end the Indian Ocean slave trade. Sir Alexander Johnston, President of His Majesty's Council and Chief Justice of Sri Lanka (1806–1819), adopted various measures to raise the political, moral, and intellectual character of the people. He obtained a charter from the Crown to extend the right of sitting upon juries to all Sri Lankans—a privilege not pos-

sessed by any other Asian nation. In return, he urged the gradual abolition of domestic slavery in Sri Lanka. Then the proprietors of domestic
slaves came to a resolution that all children born of their slaves after 12
August 1806 (the birthday of the then Prince Regent who later became
King George IV was chosen so that the slaves would associate the freedom of their descendants with reverence to the Crown), should be freed,
thereby ending the domestic slavery that prevailed in Sri Lanka for three
centuries.

William Wilberforce and Thomas Clarkson were leading campaigners
for the abolition of the slave trade in Britain. For twenty years,
Wilberforce was the British parliamentary leader of the Abolitionist
movement. After the 1807 Act, British captains were fined £100 for
every slave found on board their ships. This Act did not, however, pre-
vent British slavery, as the captains would throw the slaves into the sea
if they anticipated that the British navy would detect them. Therefore it
became necessary to make slavery illegal. A new Anti-Slavery Society
was formed in 1823. In 1833, a month after the death of Wilberforce, the
British parliament passed the "Slavery Abolition Act." Thereafter compensation was paid to the slave owners. Proposed a quarter of a century
earlier, Bertolacci's solution to the problem was finally implemented by
the British. The abolition of slavery in the British empire created an
acute shortage of labor supply. This demand was met by a new innovation—indentured laborers—and by Asians, displaced across the Indian
Ocean in a westward direction. In 1840, the British and the Omani ruler
signed a treaty that made the sale of slaves to India a crime (Beachey
1976:51-53).

In Sri Lanka, according to the British, slaves remained the legal property of their owners until the abolition of slavery. Slavery was abolished
in Sri Lanka during the Governorship of Edward Barnes (1824-31), and
a group of slave-owners in Galle and Jaffna freed all children born of
their slaves. In 1841, an ordinance was passed to abolish the last vestiges
of slavery on the Island. In 1845, Lord Stanley executed the final act of
the extinction of slavery. Slave-owners did not receive compensation;
nor did they demand it.

There is some public awareness of the slave trade, as suggested by place names such as Slave Island. Although it is now a busy commercial area in Colombo, during Sri Lanka's colonial era, slaves brought by the European colonizers were housed there. Detailed research is needed on the events that followed the Abolition and its effects on the freed slaves. More (1827), a leading member of the British Abolitionist movement, published a play titled *The Feast of Freedom* which was written to commemorate the Abolition. The celebrated composer and performer Charles Wesley adapted the vocal parts of the play to music. *The Feast of Freedom* has been translated into many Indian languages, having been originally translated into Sinhala by two Buddhist priests. The names of characters (Cingalese) and commodities (cinnamon and coconut) indicated strong Sri Lankan elements in the play (de Silva Jayasuriya 2001a).

The political, communication, legal, and military infrastructure required for trade, both locally and globally, by empires have been financed by a variety of methods—taxation, custom duties, and the creation of state monopolies. The flow of commodities, including African slaves, has been central to the prosperity of empire. Long-distance forced migration of Africans resulted from western commercial expansion overseas and colonization. The relationship between commodity markets and empires appears to be fairly obvious: imperial powers were profit-driven.

CHAPTER 4

The Military Role of Africans

One of the key roles that Africans who went eastward played was within the military. As outsiders with no filial connections to Asians, they were sought after as soldiers. The use of foreign troops was a military strategy common to many monarchs and rulers. Africans were favored as soldiers not only due to their loyalty but also because of their physical strength and courage. Due to the long distances over which they were transported from their homelands and the sociopolitical changes that occurred after their transportation, African slave-soldiers and trained military men were often trapped in Asia. In this chapter, some examples will be used to illustrate how Africans demonstrated their military capabilities in several Asian countries at various times.

African Soldiers and Bodyguards

The military strength of Africans was established many centuries ago. In the second and fourth centuries, Ethiopian armies invaded Southern Arabia and occupied it from 335 to 370. Ethiopia invaded Yemen again in 524. In 532, Abraha, an Ethiopian general who led the invasion to Yemen, seized the South Arabian throne with the support of Ethiopian soldiers who wanted to settle in Yemen. Abraha's sons by a Yemeni woman became his successors.

An important feature of Islamic civilization was the military role of slaves; it had considerable repercussions on foreign and domestic policy in several Muslim states (Pipes 1981). The Zanj revolted against the

Caliphate several times. The first of these insurrections occurred in Basra, from 689 to 690. This was, however, suppressed. The next rebellion, led by Riyāh, known as "the lion of the Zandj," occurred in 694. It could only be suppressed with the reinforcement of the Caliphal army by volunteers from Basra (Talib and Samir 1989:726). The revolt of 869 lasted more than fourteen years and was led by an Arab, Alī b. Muhammed (Popovic 1976:71-81). After African slaves had demonstrated their military might during the rebellion in Iraq, they were sought after by the Abbasid Caliph in 813, and a special corps of Ethiopian bodyguards called "Crows" was formed (Al-Sābi 1958:6). In 932, during the reign of al-Mukadir, no fewer than 7,000 Africans fought for the Caliph during the fierce battle for power. After 825, Africans in the Abbasid army of Iraq decreased. The Abbasid Empire was one of the world's most powerful empires at its height, presiding directly over Iraq, Mesopotamia, and western Persia and indirectly over territories from North Africa to Central Asia and from the Caspian Sea to the Red Sea (Popovic 1999:xi).

In the northwestern Indian Ocean, African sailors served in military retinues; the majority of them were involuntary migrants, but some were free. The Islamic world—from Spain to Bengal—engaged Africans as militia. The ruler owned military slaves, who were generally older children or adults. Boys aged twelve were preferred as it took several years of training to become good soldiers and it was easier to inculcate a sense of loyalty in them.

Eunuchs were carried from North African ports to all the courts of the Ottoman Empire, including Istanbul, Mecca, and Medina. They rose to positions of importance in Arabian societies and became the keepers of the *Kaaba*, a religious shrine in Mecca (Marmon 1995). African eunuchs served in India's Muslim courts and Indian paintings from Deccani, Rajput, and Mughal testify to this (Robbins and McLeod 2006). However, castrated Africans were needed to watch the women in the harems. Some African military men were eunuchs. The survival rate of castrated Africans was low and eunuchs were highly respected. Although they were foreigners, they were trusted and taken to the intimate parts of the Sultanate. Unfortunately, after they died, they were often forgotten since they did not leave behind any children.

In addition, Bacharach (1981:471) draws attention to the differences in the Turkish military. Africans and African military men were held in low esteem at that time. In 695, racial tensions were probably heightened after the revolt at Basra, Iraq. By the ninth century, prejudices surfaced and stereotypes appear to have existed vis-à-vis Africans in nearby eastern Islamic countries. The military positions of the two groups reflected and reinforced racial differences—cavalry was superior to infantry; Turk was superior to African.

Between 1503 and 1508, an Italian traveler, Ludovico di Varthema, noted that at Zeila, a port in the Gulf of Aden, "a very great number of slaves, which are those people of Prester John whom the Moors take in battle, and from this place they are carried into Persia, Arabia Felix and to Mecca, Cairo and into India" (Jones 1863:86). This indicates that Abyssinians were a military force fighting for the Arabs and moving from country to country with them. Significantly, most such records provide no details of payment to the soldiers. As a result, it is uncertain whether they were mercenary soldiers who were paid for fighting or they were receiving non-monetary payments or simply serving their masters due to enslavement.

Moreover, in the Persian Gulf, the practice of using slaves as soldiers was common. Historical evidence suggests that in eighteenth-century Iran, Africans reached high administrative positions. In 1717, Ya'qūb Sultan, an African slave, became the Governor of Bandar Abbas which was the main port serving central and southern Iran. Shah Sultan Husayn, who died in 1722, visited the Isfahan markets with his retinue during the first days of the Iranian New Year. He had an equal number of white and black eunuchs—one hundred of each.

Habshi Leaders

Given that the Abyssinians had established reputations as guardians of the Indian Ocean, it is not surprising that they rose to positions of leadership in Asia. In thirteenth-century India, Raziya, the Queen of the Delhi Sultanate, appointed an Abyssinian slave, Jalal-ud-din Yaqut, to be the master of the royal stable which was an important position. The Africans were known for their equestrian skills and their ability to train wild horses. Clearly, this was an asset to them as soldiers. This remains of interest since Bacharach (1981) found a different scenario in the Middle East, as explained above.

In Sri Lanka, Ibn Batuta, the fourteenth-century Moroccan traveler, noted that Jalasti, the ruler of Colombo, had 500 Abyssinians in his garrison (Gibb 1929). Batuta also recorded that the Governor of Alapur (north of Delhi) was an African (Gibb 1929:229-230). From Batuta's records, it is apparent that Abyssinians were established as soldiers even at that time. Batuta carried fifty Abyssinians on board his ship as they were "the guardians of safety on the Indian Ocean." Batuta also noted that Habshi slaves had passed into Indian legend due to their bravery. This is significant, as it clearly shows that the Portuguese and other Europeans followed established practice in the Indian Ocean and continued to engage Abyssinians, who were the best soldiers at that time.

In addition, Abyssinians governed the kingdom of Bengal in northeastern India; they were valuable knights and waited upon the kings in their apartments (Pires 1944:88). In the fifteenth century, Rukn-ud-din Barbak, the King of Bengal, had 8,000 African slave-soldiers in his army. In 1490, another king of Bengal, Habesh Khan, became dictatorial, and Sidi Badr, an African guardsman seized the throne and ruled for over three years; he was known as Shams-ud-din Abu Nasr Musaffar Shah (Obeng 2007a:275). No fewer than 5,000 Abyssinians served in his army; this was a significant number, considering that the total army consisted of 30,000 men. In 1493, he was murdered, and Africans in high positions were expelled from Bengal, marking the end of an era (Marjumdar 1960:345–346). These Abyssinians drifted to the Deccan and Gujarat, and many of them found employment as mercenaries (Sadiq Ali 1996:31; Khalidi 1988:6–7). Two sixteenth-century Portuguese chroniclers, João de Barros and Tomé Pires, mention Milic Dastur, an Abyssinian slave of the King of Deccan, who was an important person in the kingdom. His land had bordered the Narsinga frontier, and he lived in the Kulbarga with his garrison (Pires 1944:51).

John Huygen van Linschoten (1855:264–5), the sixteenth-century

Dutch traveler, who wrote about the people he saw in India, stated that there were many *Abexiins* (Abyssinians) in India at that time. Some were Muslims while others were Christians of the Ethiopian Orthodox Church. He mentions that many Ethiopians had been brought as slaves and captives and then sold. The Christian Ethiopians had four burnt marks on their faces, in the manner of a cross, which were made at baptism. These Abyssinians had been sailors, moving from Goa to China, Japan, Bengal, Malacca, Hormuz, and other places in the East. The Portuguese, who worked as sailors in the ships sailing from Lisbon to India, considered their tasks demeaning, as they wanted to be masters of the ships—captains and *Chief Botesonnes* (Chief Boatswains) (Linschoten 1855:266–7). The ship's captain bargained with its owners and received the monthly wages for his crew.

In India, Africans ruled non-Africans. Slaves derived power from their proximity to the ruling elite. Royal slaves were often used to control independent constellations of power inside the court, since it centralized power in the hands of the ruler.

Abyssinians built a chain of fortresses on the west coast of India, from Diu to the island of Janjira, which is south of Mumbai, so that they could dock nearby and control access to the coast from the sea. In 1559, the Portuguese took Daman from Sidi Bofeta (Moniz 2000:3). In 1561–2, however, the Portuguese had to retreat before the combined forces of Sidi Marium and Sidi Elal of Diu. Malik Ambar, the most famous of Habshi commanders, was Ethiopian-born and sold into slavery. He changed ownership several times before he came to India as a slave to Chengiz Khan, the *Peshwa* (Minister) of Ahmednagar. Ambar subsequently became the Peshwa of Ahmednagar (1600 to 1626). Malik Ambar built up an African army, which began with only 150 men but increased to 7,000 (Sarhar 1955:6–7). In 1610, William Finch, an English merchant who was in Burhanpur, north of Ahmednagar, reported on "Amber-champon, an Abashed [Habshi] and generall of the King of Decans forces with some ten thousand of his own cost [caste], all brave souldiers, and som forty thousand Deccanees" (Foster 1968:138). Finch's use of the word "cost" (caste) for Abyssinians in India illustrates how Africans were perceived as a separate group, similar to a "caste"; however, they were not part of the caste system. The Indian word *jāti* was the indigenous word and can be translated as race or kind. Portuguese initially used the word *casta*—and other westerners, who followed them into Asia, borrowed this word from them.

While Malik Ambar is acknowledged in Indian historiography, the roles that other Africans played in the military field are not well recognized. Through military service, Africans were able to make significant contributions to the state and thereby achieve recognition. It appears that there was a tradition of freed slaves purchasing Africans for their own personal armies.

Ambar was associated with the Nizam Shahi dynasty which began in 1496 with Ahmad I and ended in 1636 with Shah Jahan annexing the Ahmednagar Sultanate to the Mughal Empire. As peshwa, Malik Ambar controlled his puppet sultans between 1595 and 1626, when his power was at its zenith. His daughter was assimilated into the royal household, becoming the wife of Sultan Murtaza II. His son Fateh Khan married the daughter of a free Habshi, Yaqut Khan, who was one of the most powerful nobles in the kingdom. Affinal relationships strengthened military and political power. Marriages were usually never contracted after romantic encounters; they were deliberate and calculated.

During the reign of Akbar (1556–1605), the Mughal empire invaded India from Afghanistan in 1526 and then consolidated and expanded. When Aurangzeb expanded the Mughal Empire and conquered Golkonda (India) in 1686, an African Princess, Ma Saheba or Bari Sahiba, had commanded a female guard that included armed African and Turkish girls (Ali 1996:147). As was evident in late seventeenth-century India, even African women demonstrated their military potential. The Mughal Empire reached its zenith in the eighteenth century, when it expanded into Kabul and Kashmir in the subcontinent.

During Mughal rule (1526–1739) of India, a Habshi navy was based in Surat, the most important harbor in Gujarat at the time. These African seamen accompanied pilgrims to Mecca and offered protection to the travelers. While the history of elite soldiers has been recorded, the courage of numerous African slaves, who were brought to India until the end of the nineteenth century, remains unknown.

A few Africans were brought to the Carnatic coast. When the nawab (ruler) died in 1855, there were only twenty Habshis, all of them born in the Madras area (Ali 1966:236). The Nawab of Carnatic had African Cavalry—and Abyssinian horsemen accompanied him when he traveled to offer protection.

According to Kamar Badshah, an elder of the Afro-Gujaratis, their ancestors were bodyguards in the palace; they often tasted the Maharajah's food before he indulged in his meal (Catlin-Jairazbhoy and Alpers 2004:7). This may have been to ensure that the Maharajah was protected if the food was poisoned. It could also have been to check if it was palatable. Moreover, it could also have been to test the loyalty of the bodyguards.

Obeng (2007a:272) reports that a retired Lieutenant Colonel in Old Goa told him about African guards who served in the Portuguese army from 1850 to 1960. From Mozambique, African soldiers were recruited to Goa (Khalidi 1988). The Portuguese moved Africans from one colony to another. Africans in Brazil and Mozambique were moved to Goa. This is of significance from the cultural contact point of view, as it implies that both West and East African cultural elements made an impression in Goa. Until 1961, when India took over the Portuguese colony of Diu, Mozambican soldiers were kept there, which was typical practice for the Portuguese who often moved their personnel from one colony to another.

African Cavalry Guards

In Hyderabad (Andhra Pradesh), African soldiers served in the nizam's army and enjoyed privileged positions in the society since they had secure jobs. In 1948, political changes that occurred after India's independence favored indigenous men as candidates for the army. In Andhra Pradesh today, there are people of African descent; they are ex-military people, now living in army barracks. In Mahboobneger, the Raja of Wanaparthy, who lived about one hundred kilometers from the city of Hyderabad, gathered the Africans who were already in the region and imported more men from East Africa. He also bought some slaves from Bombay in the 1850s (Khalidi 2006:248). These Africans were organized into two regiments—the African Bodyguard and an African cavalry, which was later named the Wanaparthy Lancers and subsequently called the Golconda Lancers. A dispute broke out between the Raja and the nizam—and the British intervention led to a peace treaty, when the Raja gifted the African Bodyguard and the African cavalry to the nizam.

The instability that followed India's independence in 1947 had a lasting effect on the African men. The princely states and the nizam's army were disbanded after the Police Action of 1949 to 1951. The soldiers were given a pension and retired. Although the sudden change in their employment was convenient for the administrators, the soldiers were ill-prepared to perform any other tasks. They were unprepared for what could be called the "Early Retirement Scheme" that was forced upon them. A few of them became *khanasads* (household boys) in the nizam's palace where they were given the bare necessities of life; they were fed and clothed as part of the palace retinue.

Soldiers in Colonial Armies

The Portuguese practice of using African slaves as sailors (*marinheiros*) and soldiers (*soldados*) was quite understandable. The voyages to their newly-founded maritime outposts cost many lives. Disease on board, malnutrition, and shipwreck added to the time spent on voyages, which was further lengthened by currents in the high seas. Walker (2006:240) states that the slave-soldiers served the Portuguese elite in the East, adding that these soldiers often fought beside their masters or owners as well.

The three consecutive European colonizers of Sri Lanka—Portuguese (1505–1658), Dutch (1658–1796), British (1796–1948)—brought Africans to supplement their forces. Thus far evidence suggests that African soldiers were brought to Sri Lanka by the Portuguese from Goa. In Sri Lanka, African soldiers, who were sent from Goa, rescued the Portuguese from an early defeat (de Silva Jayasuriya 2001c). Gravely concerned about the situation in Sri Lanka, the Portuguese Viceroy sent aid to Dom

Jorge de Almeida (Portuguese Captain-General from 1631 to 1633 and from 1635 to 1636) so that he could recover the lost territories. Close to defeat, the Portuguese were restricted to three forts in the kingdom of Kōtte—Colombo, Galle, and Negombo. At that time, Sri Lanka was divided into three kingdoms: Kōtte, Jaffnapatam, and Kandy.

On 6 October 1631, two *pataxos* with 337 Canarese and 100 Kaffirs were sent from Goa to join de Almeida at Cochin with instructions to proceed to Sri Lanka. On 13 October 1631, four other ships carrying supplies of food, money, munitions, eighty Portuguese, 800 Canarese, and 200 Kaffirs sailed directly from Goa to Colombo. In Sri Lanka, the Kaffir contingent in the Portuguese army appeared after 1631. The African soldiers received monetary rewards. De Silva (1972) lists the fixed annual expenditure of Kōtte from 1617 to 1638, which shows the total cost associated with the Kaffirs as 5,208 xerafims. The cost of mats and ropes that were used to bundle 1350 bahars of cinnamon and for clothes of the Kaffirs was 700 xerafims; the salary of 280 Kaffirs at one fanam a day cost 1,708 xerafims; and the rice allowance for 280 Kaffirs of two measures a day cost 2,800 xerafims.

In 1622, African slaves defended the Portuguese base in Macau which the Dutch attacked with a force of thirteen ships and 1300 men. The Portuguese only had fifty trained musketeers and 100 residents, many of whom were *mestiços* on their side. They were aided by Jesuit artillerists and about fifty to hundred slaves who were given arms for defense. Quite surprisingly, the Dutch suffered a bad defeat with the loss of many men and high-ranking officials. The Portuguese only lost six lives and twenty-six of their men were wounded. Jan Pieterzoon Coen, the Dutch commander, underwent a learning experience at this battle. He advised that slaves should be used as soldiers instead of Dutch troops—and noted that it was the Portuguese slaves, Kaffirs, and others, who beat the Dutch (Boxer 1968:85).

In the same year, the Portuguese were attacked in the Persian Gulf. Africans, mostly Bantu slaves, threw explosive fire bombs from the ramparts onto the enemy. Although the Portuguese lost Hormuz in May 1622, they were able to stand up to Anglo-Persian attacks on their fortress at Hormuz (Boxer 1968:85-86).

When Captain-General Diego de Mello de Castro led the Portuguese in Sri Lanka (from 1633 to 1635 and again from 1636 to 1638) in the attack of Kandy on 27 March 1638, his force included 300 Kaffirs. After the Portuguese were dislodged from the Island by the Dutch, some Kaffirs served under the Dutch; others had settled down in the Kandyan kingdom which had remained under Sinhalese rule. Records suggest that they were greatly valued by the Sinhalese monarch and employed as personal bodyguards. Rāja Sinha II (1635–87), the monarch of the Kandyan kingdom, had a "guard of *Cofferies* or Negroes in whom he imposeth more confidence then in his own People. These are to watch at his chamber door, and next his person" (Knox 1681:56).

Mundy (1907) referred to seeing Africans with the Portuguese at Macau in October 1637. He (1907:266) mentioned the *Cavalleros* (Cavaliers), "each having their Negroes or Caphers [*kafir*] clad in Damaske, an ordinary wear For slaves and servauntts. These carried lances with pendants, wheron were painted their Masters Armes, butt when they came to [the game of] Alcansias each negro served his Master...."

In 1640, 100 Kaffir archers fought for the Portuguese against the Dutch in Galle (Southern Province) (De Silva 1972). On 13 March 1640, the Dutch seized Galle—and some Kaffirs and Canarese were retained to repair the ramparts. In 1644, when the Portuguese were defending Negombo fort against the Dutch, Dom Philippo de Mascarenhas (the Portuguese Captain General from 1630 to 1631 and again from 1640 to 1645) had 300 Kaffirs in his force (de Silva 1953). Pieris (1973) describes the Dutch defeat of the Portuguese in Jaffnapatam, where "300 armed *Toupas* and *Kaffirs* ... and 1200 sick people, slaves ..." emerged from the fort. In 1656, after the Dutch took control of Colombo, the slaves of the Portuguese were taken prisoner. Two Portuguese generals and the son of António de Sousa Coutinho, the Portuguese Captain-General (1655–56), were allowed to remove their property, including their slaves and servants. The slaves owned by the other Portuguese were confiscated, save for a few exceptions. The *Casados* (Portuguese-married soldiers) were allowed to immigrate to Goa but they were not allowed to take their property and slaves with them.

As a chaplain, Baldaeus accompanied Rickloff van Goens in the 1658 expedition against Mannar and Jaffnapatam. His is therefore an eye-witness account. Though the Dutch captured Colombo in 1656, at which point the Portuguese era (1505–1658) is generally considered to have ended, the Dutch were not at ease until they finally drove out the Portuguese from the northern part of the island two years later. Baldaeus (Brohier 1960) describes the ceding of the Fort of Saint George in Mannar. Among the Portuguese prisoners in the Mannar fort was a Kaffir who was a Captain and had made a fuss about his rank, refusing to bear arms or to do other kinds of labor; he insisted that he would rather submit himself to a sound thrashing than degrade himself so. When the Portuguese were driven out of Sri Lanka by the Dutch, some Kaffirs simply swapped masters; others settled down in the Kandyan kingdom which had remained under Sinhalese rule. Pieris also mentions that the personal guard of the Sinhalese king, Rājasinha (1635–1687), was composed of Kaffirs. This illustrates how Africans were chosen for the most trustworthy positions. Bertolacci (1817) remarked that though 9,000 Kaffirs had been brought for the regiments in Sri Lanka, their presence was not known at that time.

Portuguese moved slave-soldiers, who trained in Brazil by fighting the Dutch in South America, to Goa. Although this appears to be a long journey, the practice continued until the end of the nineteenth century, by which time the Portuguese would have been desperate to hang on to their holdings in the East; in the seventeenth century, they had lost their supremacy in the Indian Ocean, with only a few enclaves remaining. The use of African soldiers was common practice in Diu (in Gujarat today), which the Portuguese held from 1535 until India took it over in 1961. A colonial administrator noted that the Portuguese garrison in Diu mostly consisted of Africans (Pearson 1990:95).

In 1760, the British garrison in Bombay included 661 Africans (Edwardes 1910:262). In 1804, when the British were in the deep throes of the Napoleonic War, they contracted some ninety-one African soldiers from the Portuguese camp in Goa to be sent to Sri Lanka so that the soldiers could be trained in the British camps. At that time, the British were holding forth on the coastal areas (Shirodkar 1985:36–37). In 1808, the Portuguese Viceroy in Goa obtained permission from Lisbon to buy African slaves so that he could relieve navy crewmen who were patrolling the Indian Ocean. However, the Portuguese had yet to abolish the slave trade at that time.

In Sri Lanka, the British had two regiments that included Africans. In the nineteenth century, there were 874 Africans in the third and fourth Ceylon regiments. In 1796, the British took over the Maritime Provinces from the Dutch and colonized the coastal areas until 1815, when they were able to acquire the Kandyan kingdom after a third attempt. During the initial decades on the island, the British needed good soldiers. They only inherited the maritime areas from the Dutch, but they brought the entire island under their rule. By the end of the mid-nineteenth century, maintaining many garrisons proved to be uneconomical.

Hardy (1864) mentioned 6,000 Kaffir soldiers in Sri Lanka. Given the number of African soldiers who served in Sri Lanka, it is not surprising that an African weapon, *Hasagaey*, was introduced (de Silva 1972:188).

Ghanaian Soldiers in Indonesia

The Dutch colonial army recruited West Africans to serve in the East Indies. For them, the Ashantis were a source of manpower, and they enjoyed cordial relationships with them. After the British Abolition Act of 1807, this recruitment had to be done in a subtle manner, as explained in Chapter 3. No fewer than 2,200 Africans were recruited by the Dutch colonial army between 1831 and 1842. Almost 800 Ghanaians were recruited into the Dutch colonial army between 1860 and 1872. Kasruri (2002:144) points out that the Ghanaians recruited to the Dutch army were prisoners of war who were tributes to the Ghanaian king, having been owed by conquered territories. This kind of activity only ceased when the Dutch possessions on the Guinea Coast were transferred to Britain in 1872 (Van Kessel 2007:246). Indonesians called them *Belinda Hitam* (Black Dutchmen), and they were part of the Dutch colonial "machinery." When Indonesia regained independence in 1965, these soldiers, who were Dutch citizens, returned to Holland.

African Soldiers in World War II

An article by a Tanganyika district officer, who went to India and Burma with the Duke of Devonshire in the 1940s, gives us an idea of the high esteem in which African troops were held during World War II. It demonstrates how the British authorities considered the welfare of the East African Askari (from the Persian word *askar* which means "soldier") and even wondered if their wives should be allowed to accompany them. In 1942, the reputation of Japanese soldiers caused concern to the British since the Indian and British units had been unsuccessful in fighting them. In addition, Africans had defeated the best Blackshirt Italians. The first East African troops sailed to Sri Lanka (Ceylon) in 1942. After a period of intensive training on the island, the troops were taken to Chittagong (Bangladesh) and then on to Myanmar (Burma). At this time, both East African troops and West African divisions, the eighty-first and ninety-second, were active. Sabben-Clare (1945:154) stated that the admirable achievements of these Africans in the Far East should not be forgotten, in a complete written account of the African troops. The British authorities doubted if any other troops could have achieved what the Africans had—East Africans went through the Kabaw Valley and West Africans braved the tidal creeks and swamps of the Arakan. Before World War II in 1939, there were less than 20,000 Africans, both western and eastern, in the British forces. The war, however, changed the pattern of African recruitment. As many as 120,000 Africans were in the Burma campaign. Like in the Turkish situation, the ability of Africans as cavalrymen was doubted. Pre-war African units were mainly infantry. The pressures of war, however, appear to have changed traditional thinking. Earlier, it was considered that to train a cavalryman took many years. The war altered the pattern of recruiting from a few tribes with reputations for courage and military skills. The British discovered that previously untapped areas of West Africa, namely southern Nigeria, provided the most able soldiers. From East Africa, nevertheless, almost every tribe was recruited. The British need to defeat the enemy worked in favor of the Africans.

Military Skills and Social Mobility

Around the tenth century, Turks had a reputation for being excellent cavalrymen while Africans were better at infantry. Africans did not appear to have had a tradition of horsemanship at that time, but at a later time in India the situation was different. Bacharach (1981:472) points out that a change in military strategy altered the demand for Africans. At that time, there were as many as 20,000 African cavalrymen and 30,000 African infantrymen.

In India, Africans were appointed as admirals in Mughal fleets. When their master died, African slave-soldiers and free lancers (slaves who had become free) served in the Deccan. Africans from Bengal migrated to Gujarat, Deccan, and other parts of India, after their African-led rule ended. Patel (2004:213) states that Afro-Indians came to India as soldiers in the invading Muslim armies. Moreover, Africans served in several local armies including those in Kathiawar and Kutch (Wilberforce-Bell 1916; Tambs-Lyche 1997).

Indian monarchs were under continuous threat from their neighboring states and rival heirs—and this created a demand for good and loyal soldiers. Since the loyalty of Indian soldiers was dubious, the gap in the labor market was filled by the Africans. In particular, it created a demand for African males. Although India was hardly short on human capital, Africans had a comparative advantage in the defense sector. Most Africans were probably involuntary migrants; however, some of them were able to break into the power hierarchy and thereby gain position and prestige in India.

The Portuguese moved Africans from one part of their empire to another. Mozambicans and Angolans were sent to Timor, Macau, Goa, Daman, and Diu. Africans from Goa were sent to Sri Lanka. In Sri Lanka, when the Portuguese withdrew, these Africans changed their masters or employers/patrons. However, the change of European powers in the Indian Ocean did not alter the demand for African soldiers. Some soldiers crossed over to the indigenous army and served Sri Lankan kings.

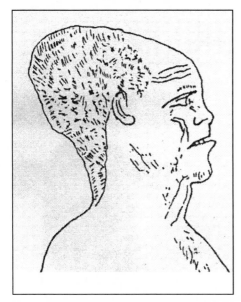

Joseph Fernando:
An Afro-Sri Lankan
(Source: *Journal of the*
Royal Asiatic Society [Ceylon], 1918)

Unlike in India where Habshi commanders were deemed important and are depicted in Indian paintings as legends, the achievement of Africans in Sri Lanka, such as those of Joseph Fernando, is less acknowledged. Fernando assisted the Kandyan army in fending off the British forces and delaying them from gaining control of the Kandyan kingdom—and this was not an easy task.

In some cases, military duties worked out well, offering Africans social mobility, as they excelled and rose to leadership roles. However, there were many who were not as successful. When the balance of power tipped, ordinary soldiers were usually left behind. The western colonizers eventually returned to Europe or to another part of their empire. Sometimes the soldiers were retired with monetary payments, but they were ill-prepared for any other type of work and gradually marginalized in society.

Although the Ghanaians may not have voluntureed to join the Dutch army, they nevertheless enjoyed a European standard of living in Indonesia and intermarried with the Euro-Indonesians and Indonesians. Their houses were sturdy and well-built—and they even had Javanese servants. Soldiers were recruited at around the age of sixteen and retired at thirty. They were given the option of returning to Ghana; many settled down in Elmina with a plot of land allocated to them by the Dutch governor. A few of them remained in the East Indies with their extended families and founded the Afro-Indonesian communities of Purworejo,

Semarang, Salatiga, and Solo (Van Kessel 2002:133). When Indonesia regained independence in 1949, they repatriated to the Netherlands. In 1956, those who had remained behind also moved to the Netherlands with the second wave of immigration.

CHAPTER 5

Sounds of Africa

A frican migrants have made their presence known in many parts of the world through the sounds of their music. The Mardi Gras in New Orleans, soul music in Afro-Caribbean London, and the two-week annual festival in Rio de Janeiro ring out sounds of African identity.

Like language, music is a signifying practice with its own characteristics; it is a socially and culturally constituted form of human expression and knowledge that gives rise to effects and meanings specific to particular sets of historical contingencies (Shepherd and Wicke 1997:3). Music illustrates the patterns of African migration in the Middle East and the Indian subcontinent. Perhaps due to the circumstances under which most Africans migrated, they could only take music and dance with them. In many cases, even African languages have not survived.

In this chapter, I will explore the music of displaced peoples and what it can inform us about their past. The African presence in Asia has remained concealed from both scholars and Asians themselves. Many migrants carried their musical traditions with them to their new homes. These traditions are particularly important among African migrants in Asia, who have or are assimilating to their host countries. My hypothesis is that music and dance are among the best indicators of an African legacy. I will consider case studies from the Islamic Gulf states, India, Pakistan, Sri Lanka, and the Maldives to test this hypothesis.

In Africa, visual, musical and dramatic arts work together and are conceptually treated as intertwined (Stone 1998:7). In several African societies, music and oral literature are inseparable. Song texts or "talking drums" (the drumming of poetry based on the tonality of language) and storytelling with songs as a community-oriented event involving relatively few people are common practices. The orality of African music implies that a certain range of variation can often be expected from one performance of the same song to another. The composers of African music were forgotten due to the lack of historical consciousness; songs were generally transmitted independently of the composer, then picked up, adapted, and reinterpreted by other musicians. However, this is not limited to African music only. African musicians try to produce at least two rhythms simultaneously. The juxtaposing of opposing rhythms characterizes African music. Usually, African rhythms combine two and three meters, which often sound at the same time, to form polyrhythms. Lévi-Strauss (1972:210) posits that the meaning of music cannot be found in the isolated elements of music—only in the manner in which these elements are combined.

Since Africans in Asia have gone unnoticed for so long, it is necessary to first identify those with African roots before musical traditions could be further researched (de Silva Jayasuriya 2006c). There are some important factors that one should take into account when analyzing African music. The word "music" (from the Latin word *musica*) has no semantic equivalent in African languages; however, there are words for singing, playing instruments, and performing. Isolating musical sounds from other forms of art is a western abstraction. In Africa, there is song instead of music, reflecting perhaps that African instrumental melodies "speak" and can be verbalized. In African instrumental ensembles, the concept of blending is largely subservient to contrasting. Each instrument is distinctly audible and retains its independent identity. Given the main principles of African music—that is, meaning depends on conflict of rhythms and meters, and on the interplay between musicians and instruments—African musicians are aware of quality of tone and its subtle differences. African languages rarely describe music in terms of time.

The Middle East

During the medieval era, Africans continued to arrive as slaves in Muslim Asia. Islamic law prohibited the enslavement of fellow Muslims. Children who were born to a Muslim master and his female slave were considered free. Therefore, Arab Muslims sought slaves from non-Muslim regions of Europe, Asia, and Africa. Slaves worked as musicians, household servants, palace eunuchs, skilled workers, and soldiers in Arabia.

The Portuguese bought slaves from the Swahili Coast as they required manpower for their settlements in Africa and India. After 1650, Oman became a major trading partner for the Swahili ports, especially in the Lamu Archipelago. During the first few decades of the eighteenth century, the Omanis were trading slaves from the Swahili Coast or the Yao. Slaves were acquired for labor in the plantations of Oman. Alpers (1997) draws attention to African musical traditions in Oman that can be traced to specific regions of Northeast and East Africa.

In the Basra region of southern Iraq—Kuwait, Bahrain, Oman, and also the United Arab Emirates—people of East African origin perform tanburah. This tradition is named after the lyre (*tanburah*) which is used in the ritual. The performance could be a weekly social occasion or a special ritual to treat illness caused by spirit possession. Women or men dance in rows, accompanied by an ensemble of lyre, several single-headed cylindrical drums, and a *manjur* (a rattle belt made from animal hooves) (Racy 2002). Thawra Youssef, an Iraqi who recalls oral histories of her family's connections with slavery in Kenya, has prepared a dissertation on healing ceremonies for the University of Basra in Iraq. She is aware that her ancestors had left Kenya as slaves. Basra was a major trading city—and the Arabs had turned to Mombasa on the Kenyan coast, Sudan, Tanzania, Malawi, and Zanzibar to gain the supply of labor required for date plantations and salt marshes. These ceremonies were held exclusively for dark-skinned Iraqis in Basra and served a variety of functions: to cure the sick, cure people suffering from physical ailments (*Shtanga* ceremony), remember the dead, and enjoy occasions such as weddings. Another ceremony called *nouba* is named after Nubia; it was considered a dramatic performance and included singing songs that had Swahili and Arabic lyrics and dancing. According to Sunni Khalid, a freelance journalist, *haywa*, a popular dance in Basra and Kuwait, could also have East African origins. In addition, spillovers to Classical Iraqi music might have occurred, as some compositions by the late Munir Bashir are apparently based on the African-influenced music of southern Iraq.

In Oman, the *bayt al-zar* (house where the *zar* or spirit possession ceremony is held), is empty and often far from any settlement or beach. Its only function is to serve as a place where zar takes place (Christensen 2002). Both men and women face a rocking figure which is veiled in a green cloth. Two large drums are played in an even, unaccented rhythm, which signals that a healing ritual has begun. A man waves incense around the veiled figure while reciting—and the men and women respond to him in chorus. This ceremony continues for hours and the sick person, who is possessed by a *jinn* (evil spirit), moves around erratically and violently. The ritual is repeated on three consecutive nights to cure the possessed person.

Alpers (2003) has also drawn attention to the African influences maintained through the widespread popularity of zar and tanburah possession cults, which are derived from Ethiopia and the Sudan. They often incorporate African spirits, African musical instruments and rhythms, African dance forms, and African songs whose meanings are usually unintelligible to modern adherents of these cults. In Southern Iran, for example, possession has become an integral part of the local Iranian culture, afflicting the poor and dispossessed in particular; all the adepts in the cults, however, are of African descent. The most powerful and dangerous spirits were African. In coastal Iran, there were no separate black quarters, as in the larger Iranian towns. Mirzai (2005:32) notes that the practice of spirit possession ceremonies such as *zar*, *gowat*, and *liwa* were often prevalent where enslaved Africans settled in Iran.

Another category of spirits, known as *Noban* (from Nubia), has African roots. *Al-nuban*, in which singing and poetry are combined with dancing, is the main Afro-Arab musical ritual of possession and healing.

The ensemble called *iddat al-nuban* (tools of Nuba) consists of a tanbu-rah, four kettledrums, and a manjur (Hassan 2002). Zar spirits are known as *pepe* (from the Swahili word *pepo*, the generic term for any possessing spirit), *maturi* (from the Swahili word *matari*, a specific spirit), *dingmaro* (the Swahili spirit *Dungamaro*), *chinyase* (from *Cinyasa*, the language of the Nyasa people in southern Malawi who fed the slave trade of East Central Africa), and *tagruri* (a generic name for slaves from *Takrur*, the western Sudan). As part of the Iranian Islamic culture, these musical tra-ditions, which have survived until today, represent a popular conscious-ness of the African heritage in a community.

Jihad Racy (2006) points out that in the Gulf region, the tanburah is testimony to the African roots of the local community. Its pentatonic melodies and sound quality ring out a sense of the past and generate rem-iniscences of far-off places of origin. The tanburah songs often express nostalgia—or they construct impressions of another world that is experi-enced through music and dance. The dance has ethnic and historic sym-bolism. Tanburah also maintains allegiance to Islam and pays homage to Bilal, a freed Abyssinian slave who was asked by the Prophet Muham-mad to perform the first Islamic call to prayer. This displayed Bilal's devotion to Islam and his musical abilities. Although most of the lyrics of tanburah songs are in Arabic, a few African words have been retained. The tanburah is viewed as the repository of culture and traditions of the Nuban community; it reveals a sense of ethnic identity which migrants create by recalling an imagined world.

Spirit possession is a belief, a ritual and a ceremonial performance. Khalifa (2006a) examines this practice in Dubai, United Arab Emirates. She describes African zar diagnosis, ritual ceremonies, and its symbolic elements. As a belief and a practice, zar differs fundamentally from Islamic practices. Khalifa explains how, in the light of social stigma, zar was modified by Islamic practices and codes of ethics. She also discusses zar as an organization that acknowledges women as leaders and how the cult conceals aspects of its rituals and ceremonies in order to maintain the cohesiveness of the group. In addition, Khalifa connects spirit pos-session to slavery and indicates how slaves used possession, both as a form of mimicking and as a way of coping with their enslavement.

The Akdham, Hajur, and Subian are of African origin and considered to be descendants of Abyssinian invaders of Yemen from the third to sixth centuries. The maritime trade in the Indian Ocean led to cross-continental musical flows in both directions. For centuries, the coastal regions of Yemen absorbed outside cultural and musical influences from Africa, India, and the Far East, due to its strategic location on the important maritime trade routes of the Red Sea and the Indian Ocean. Yemen's significance on the trade route has resulted in Indian and Far Eastern musical flows affecting its music. Ingrams (2006) has studied the African links in Yemeni music. Somalis, Eritreans, and Ethiopians traded in Aden and also settled down there. Different musical traditions prevailed in the north and south of the country. After the revolution in 1962, the music of northern Yemen was related to military and religious purposes. The Seiyun Popular Arts Group, formed in 1963, included Yemeni artists of African origin, both men and women, who beat the drums or plucked the *zither*. In the south, religious disapproval of music had been less universal since music was encouraged by the sultans, the British colonizers, and the Marxist regime. African laborers working in the harbor, salt pans, and plantations chanted tunes; the rhythm helped them cope with the tedious work. Music plays an important role in Yemeni life—and there are a number of distinct categories of work songs associated with fishing, seafaring, cultivating, and house-building. Within these categories, one can hear and locate African influences in the rhythms and the variety of instruments, song and dance. The drummer of dhows was always an African, who set the pace for activities on board with his rhythmic drumming. In Yemenite music, the number of rhythmic instruments often exceeds the number of melodic instruments. The sonic and rhythmic functions differ, based on geography, tradition, and type of ensemble, resulting in varied effects.

Adeni and Hadhrami music, in particular, have African connections. Swahili elements are used in Hadhramaut songs. Instruments played in the Hadhramaut, such as *zamzamiyah* (harp), are also played in Zanzibar as *sunsumia*. In Yemen, spontaneous dancing with hip waggling by Somalis or Swahilis accompanies music. The music of the Tihamah is strikingly African, as there is a particularly strong relationship between the drum and the dancer. The drums are attributed special powers to exorcize the evil spirit in zar possession ceremonies. In Shaykh Othman, near Aden, the zar exorcizing ceremonies were well-known and the large drums were often beaten by African women. Singing and dancing by African men and women attracted other Yemenis to join in the performance. In Aden, the capital of Yemen, African musicians, singers, and dancers are invited to perform at weddings. This indicates the importance of African music in Yemen.

South Asia

Given the scarcity of historical records and the absence of photographs or audio-visual recordings, paintings are used to portray important aspects of African lives in Asia. A mid-seventeenth century painting illustrates an African, dressed in Moroccan clothing, playing a lyre and singing. He has been identified as Sidi Sa'd, a follower of Malik Ambar, the Abyssinian ruler of Ahmednagar (Baptiste, McLeod and Robbins 2006:20–21).

Afro-Indians are generally known as Sidis today; however, the literature also refers to them as Habshi since they were perceived to have come from Abyssinia. The Afro-Indians who live in Gujarat have internationalized their music and dance. Catlin-Jairazbhoy (2006) has discussed the process of selecting materials for the ninety-minute *Sidi Goma* international tours which began in October 2002, and the modifications and developments in the musical aspects of the program that have occurred during the ensuing period. She included musical instruments, song texts, and musical settings. The Sidis often play sacred music and dance as wandering *faqirs*, singing to the Sidi Saint, Bava Gor. They perform *dhamal*, which they call *goma*, a word whose etymon is the Swahili word *ngoma* meaning "drum" and "dance" as well.

The most significant African retention among the Sidis of India is the *malunga*, a braced musical bow, which is found in many African communities and in other parts of the African diaspora; in Brazil, it is known as *berimbao*. Sidi servants performed *ngoma* dances with drums, rattles, and shells on birthdays and at weddings in the noble courts (Basu 1993). Today, Sidis wearing animal skins and headgears of peacock feathers or other bird feathers, with painted bodies, perform a sacred traditional dance to the rhythm of the *dhamal* (small drum), *madido* (big drum), *mugarman* (footed-drum), *mai mishra* (coconut rattle), *nafir* (conch trumpet), *malunga* (musical bow), and other musical instruments. *Urs* (the death of a Muslim Saint) is celebrated over several days and provides an occasion for playing *dhamal* and dancing. A late nineteenth-century painting gives an idea of the *damal* dance performed at that time. *Damal* is performed by the goma groups in Gujarat and Karnataka. The Gujarati troupe has performed abroad. Topp-Fargion (1992:310) defines *ngoma* as an event involving music and dance.

Music appears to be the main African cultural retention in Andhra Pradesh, India, where the Hyderabad Sidis are also called *Chaush*. In 1724, the Asafiya dynasty of Hyderabad (nazims) maintained a royal guard of African slave-soldiers who entertained their masters with African songs and dances. The fathers and grandfathers of the Chaushs came to Hyderabad to become bodyguards to the former nizam. The descendants of the last nizam's African cavalry guards, who live in Hyderabad today, call themselves *Chaush*, a term which is derived from Ottoman military nomenclature. Their drum bands play African drums and are hired to play music and dance in "African ways" on special occasions such as weddings. They had learned songs which are sung in a Bantu language in Tanzania during spirit possession rituals to effect healing. When a team of American historians and anthropologists visited Andhra Pradesh some years ago, a Chaush in his fifties had performed a song that he learned from his grandfather and had danced; he, however, did not understand the words of the song. An anthropology graduate student in the group, Barbara Thompson, who had been studying spirit possession in Tanzania, surprised everyone by singing the refrain of this song. The lyrics were in a Bantu language spoken in northeastern Tanzania, Shambaa. The song was still sung commonly in the first moments of the rituals that were performed to effect healing (Alpers 2003). African retentions can also be found in Swahili words of lyrics. Minda (2007) notes that the Chaushs in Hyderabad play their traditional music for the local Christian Afro-Indians whenever they are invited to social occasions. The music groups are called *Daff* Parties. The *daff* is a round single-headed frame drum which is often linked to Muslim culture. It is used in folk music, art music, dance music, and Sufi rituals. In Africa, the daff is also played by the Swahili and Swahili/Nguja people in Dar-es-Salaam and Tabora, Tanzania.

Sidis in Karnataka play the *gumat*, the drum that is also used by other Indian musicians in Goa and by the Goan diaspora who play their folk songs. The popular folk songs of the Sidis—*Balo, Leva, Bandugia*—are replete with affection for the community, its pride and religious fervor (Chauhan 1995). According to Kassebaum and Clause (2000), the Sidis, who live in northern Karnataka and the border areas of Shimogga, have their own social structure and musical genre. These Afro-Asians are descendants of slaves who were brought to western India by Arab or European traders. In Karnataka, there are Sidis who are Hindus, Muslims, and Christians. Social dancing (*aligum kunita*) of the Muslim Sidis in Karnataka is accompanied by chanting "Ali, *ali, ali*" as they commemorate Ali, the cousin and son-in-law of the Prophet Mohammed, through dance. The dance is performed by any number of people, but usually two of the dancers are dressed in the appropriate costume—shorts, headgear made of flowers, a belt of bells—and they carry a leather belt as well. The bells provide the only accompaniment to the chant. The dancers often stop and hit themselves with the belt before starting to dance again since the self-inflicted pain is believed to heighten the religious experience. Drewal (2004:151), an anthropologist, describes the African elements in the dances of the Afro-Indians as percussive, isolated, polyrhythmic body movements, including "get-down" torso posture, syncopation, improvisation, and call-and-response.

The present number of Afro-Indians is estimated at over 50,000 with the largest numbers living in the states of Karnataka, Gujarat, and Andhra Pradesh. There are also smaller communities in Maharashtra, Madhya Pradesh, Tamil Nadu, and Uttar Pradesh. Further fieldwork and research should reveal hitherto unrecognized musical traditions in Sidi communities in India.

In the mid-nineteenth century, Burton (1992:256) described a dance in the Sindh, involving both females and males. The ladies merely advanced and retired, performing occasional pirouettes. The males simply watched and then jumped and distorted their limbs. Excited by the vibrant sounds of the kettledrums and the singing, the slaves, who were normally sober, danced violently and for a long time.

In Karachchi, the Mangopir festival is an annual event celebrated by the small Afro-Pakistani community. They are the disciples of the Sufi Saint Baba Mangopir. Abbas (2002) reported on their dance, often a ceremonious, systematic, and powerful performance. The festival attracts all ethnic groups but it has retained an African connection through the drum beats. It begins with the girls offering specially prepared food to the crocodiles that live in the pond outside the shrine. The Pakistanis do not understand the words of the songs that accompany the drum beats. According to the Afro-Pakistanis, the words are a mixture of Swahili and Baluchi.

Badalkhan (2006) comments that Baloches of African origin have retained their musical heritage, as music was a tool for liberating oneself from the daily hardships of a discriminated against and less advantageous life, and a way to express rage and suffering in a natural way. Dancing and singing were of low significance to upper-class Baloch Muslims. The musical tradition of Afro-Baloches was closely related to maritime activities. Makran Baloch maritime contacts with the eastern and northeastern African coasts lasted until the first half of the twentieth century. Many African Baloches had engaged in seafaring. A Baloch seaman, who was in his seventies now, learned the songs which had Swahili lyrics while he was in Zanzibar and other African ports. Another elderly Baloch sailor recalled how sailors from all parts of the Indian Ocean joined the drumming and dancing sessions when they were stationed in an African coastal town.

Badalkhan notes similarities between the *lewa* performed in Oman and the *laywa* in the Makran. Dieter Christensen (2002) describes the *lewa* in Oman:

Lewa groups, consisting of men who are descendants of slaves, perform for profit.... Several drums, including African-type drums called *musundu* [cf. Balochi mugulmani]; conch trumpets (*jim*) [cf. Balochi conch shell *gurr*]; and metal trays of canisters used to beat the time line.... Altogether twenty to forty people who make up the group.... Dancers and singers revolve while circling around the instrumentalists. The song texts, in poorly understood Swahili and Arabic, abound with references to East Africa and seafaring.

Lewa contains strong African connotations that are neither Arab nor Muslim. According to Badalkhan, the only difference between the traditions in the Oman and Makran is that the former leads to a trance and the latter is simply a festive and merry-making dance which does not lead to a trance. Badalkhan also describes another genre of songs called *amba*, which are work songs. The instruments that are used in both *amba* and *laywa* are the same. Both musical expressions have flourished in Balochistan due to the seafaring culture of Makran and the maritime networks of the Indian Ocean.

There is historical evidence that Ethiopians were trading in Sri Lanka during the sixth century, when the island was an emporium in the Indian Ocean; but the Afro-Sri Lankans today trace their roots back to the colonial period when the Portuguese, Dutch, and British brought their ancestors to the island. De Silva Jayasuriya (2006c; 2006d) evaluates the oral traditions of the African migrants and their descendants in Sri Lanka, retrieving the memories of the largest Afro-Sri Lankan community and exposing their roots. Negritude is expressed through a combination of music and song known as *manhas* and the spontaneous unchoreographed dancing of the Afro-Sri Lankans. There are only a limited number of manhas, as the community has not composed any new songs. Some of these songs have Portuguese etyma in their lyrics while others have borrowed words, indicating cultural contact with other peoples and shedding light on their origins and route to Sri Lanka (de Silva Jayasuriya 2005a). It has been suggested that the etymon of the word *manhas* could derive from the Portuguese word *marchinhas* ("little marches"). On the other hand, an urban, popular dance-song type in Africa, which draws from South African choral music, is called *manje*. These musical traditions have to be analyzed by taking into account any evi-

Kaffrinha Dance in Sri Lanka: Late Nineteenth Century
(Source: *Journal of the Royal Asiatic Society* [Ceylon], 1896)

dence of their African roots. However, the traditions themselves may lead to the discovery of their African origins in the absence of adequate historical records and reliable oral histories of migratory routes.

The Manhas are found mainly among the Afro-Sri Lankans, but the dancing resembles *kaffrinha*. Kaffrinha is also a form of Afro-Portuguese music and song, and nineteenth-century recordings of these songs exist. Appropriated by the island's anglicized indigenous elite in the early twentieth century, kaffrinha has had an enduring effect on *baila*, a popular genre of music in postcolonial Sri Lanka (de Silva Jayasuriya 1995a, 1996, 1997a, 1997b, 1999a, 1999b, 2000a, 2000b, 2000c, 2001b, 2003d, 2003e, 2004b, 2005c, 2005d, 2005e). All three genres are rhythm-driven, which perhaps accounts for their popularity.

Kaffrinha is often confused with baila, the most popular form of music that caught the pulse of the postcolonial nation. This confusion is not without reason. *Kaffrinha (Kaffir + nha* (which is the Portuguese diminutive)) is associated with the *Kaffirs* (an ethnonym for people of African descent in Sri Lanka) and the Portuguese. It is sometimes called *kaffrinha baila*. Ariyaratne (1999) draws attention to the Sinhalese component in modern kaffrinha. A comparison between Portuguese and African folk music would help to ascertain the Sinhalese influence in contemporary Kaffrinha. Baila (from the Portuguese word "dance") is a Lusitanian musical legacy in Sri Lanka. Kaffrinha/kaffrinha baila/baila refer to popular music, song, and dance in contemporary Sri Lanka (de Silva Jayasuriya 2004b, 2006d, 2008).

Baila is a Sri Lankan composition with incorporated elements from Portuguese and African music. Built on a western European melodic system, it is a seamless merging of musical traditions from three continents and is based on western tonal harmony. Harmonization was a feature of European music; however, when Ollington Bastianz composed *chorus baila*, harmonization had already entered Sri Lankan music through Hindustani music and the introduction of the *seraphina* (harmonium). Asymmetric and cross rhythms in baila are a feature that was introduced through African music, mainly Kaffrinha rhythms. The Afro-Sri Lankans appear to have been deeply integrated with the Europeans so it is not surprising that musical flows were fluid between the African and European music systems. Bastianz set the scene for many other talented baila singers (predominantly male), many of whom were from the western coastal belt. Since many of them were either Burghers or Roman Catholic Sinhalese, it has led some to mistakenly assume that baila is a Portuguese genre. Baila has no ethnic, religious or socioeconomic bias. A cross-cultural musical composition emerged as Sri Lankans were searching for a new postcolonial identity. Baila is a forum by which ethnic and religious boundaries may be evaded altogether. Anywhere in the world, baila sessions include Sri Lankans of varied ethnic background. Even the non-Sri Lankans join the dance—they cannot resist the rhythms and melodies of the bailas.

The following description of *Zanj* ("black African") women encapsulates the dominance of rhythm in African culture:

Dancing and beating the rhythm are engrained in their nature. And since their manner of speech is unintelligible, they are given to blowing [musical instruments] and dancing. It is said: were the Zandj to fall from heaven, they would beat the rhythm in falling. (Sangustine 1980)

African slaves were brought on Arab dhows to the Maldive Islands, until about the mid-nineteenth century. They intermarried with the indigenous Maldivians and worked mostly as *raveri* or coconut-plantation keepers. Mohamed (2006) states that freed African slaves introduced the sound of the African drums to the Maldives. Since drums are considered the quintessential African instrument, this is not surprising. *Bodu beru* (means "large drum" in Divēhi, the Indic language of the Maldivians) is a genre of music that is associated with the Africans who came to the Maldives. During a visit to the Maldives, I met the descendants of Sangoaru, an African who had been brought by a Maldivian sultan on pilgrimage to Mecca. Altogether, five slaves (Sangoaru, Laalu, Marjan, Masud, and Muizz) were purchased in Mecca by this sultan. Bodu beru is played by the descendants of Sangoaru who live in the Island of Feridu in Ari Atoll. It is also played in other islands in this Atoll as well as on Felidhoo Island in Vaavu Atoll. The drummers traditionally wore a loin cloth. Maldivians cannot understand the lyrics of the authentic songs that accompany the original bodu beru. These songs are called *babaru lava* ("negro songs"); the words may be African but further research is needed in order to validate this hypothesis. Spontaneous dancing by men crouching low is spurred by the rhythms of the drums. The shaking of shoulders and heads prevail. Men engage in duels akin to wrestlers that end in head-butting and cackling.

In the 1880s, Snouck Hurgrouje, the Dutch Orientalist, visited Mecca and commented on the Sudan slaves there. He described the weekly festivals that the Africans celebrated in Mecca on Thursday nights. It involved singing and dancing—and a performance where two or more slaves danced around with long sticks in their hands, making movements as if they were fighting (Hunwick 2004:151).

Bodu beru has now been commercialized and adapted for the tourists. Nowadays, a typical bodu beru group has three drummers, a lead singer, and a chorus of ten to fifteen men. Most songs begin slowly and increase

in tempo. A few men from the group break into unchoreographed dancing, flinging their arms and legs and swaying to the beat as the music
reaches a crescendo. Unable to resist the beat of the rhythm, the audience also joins the dances. In the Maldives today, Bodu beru is the most
popular form of music among both young and older generations. The
themes of babaru lava could be love, religion, rich men versus poor men,
enjoyment, courage, or praise of the sultan. *Babaru nisun* ("negro dance")
is performed to the beat of the bodu beru and singing of lava. The
dancers sway from side to side, and the *Divehis* (means "the islanders"
and a name used for the Maldivians), who are of non-African origin,
blacken themselves to perform the dance. The drums are two-and-a-half
feet long and made out of breadfruit or coconut wood with a goatskin
membrane on each end. These drums are not considered to be similar to
those found in Sri Lanka or India, from where some Maldivians originated, and according to Maloney (1980) they could actually come from
the "old style" Arab drums.

Evaluation

Afro-Asian music illustrates how popular culture passes from one continent to another. The vibrant and varied expressions of culture and identity are a testament to the value of music and dance in Asia. The dominance of rhythm in African music has crossed over, not only to Afro-
Asian music, but also to the popular Asian music of Sri Lanka and the
Maldives.

Music is an important element in the identity formation of African
migrants in Asia. African religious beliefs may have been replaced by
other religions in the diaspora, but African musical traditions and dance
forms have lasted, often through several centuries. Asian languages and
lingue franche have also replaced African languages. However, the lyrics
of Afro-Asian songs have retained African words. In the Middle East,
African musical traditions have survived along with spirit possession rituals. In western India, African musical traditions revolve around the
veneration of Sufi Saints. Musical traditions associated with trance and

spirit possession have continued in the Middle East and in India among Asians of African descent. However, it is important to note that spirit possession and trance are not found only among Africans, as they exist in Asia among indigenous people and in other societies as well as outside the religious traditions. Significantly, African musical traditions have survived through their link with spirit possession and exorcising ceremonies.

African religious practices are encapsulated in spirit possession ceremonies such as zar and tanburah that have survived in the diaspora and exist alongside Islamic practices. In Dubai, for example, slaves used spirit possession rituals as a way to come to terms with enslavement, and African musical traditions have survived to this day. A spirit possession cult of Hausa origin called *bori*, which is described as a "deviant" religious practice by a Muslim pilgrim from Timbuktu in 1813, was practised by Africans from central Sudan. These spirit possession cults were described as non-Muslim or even pre-Islamic but they co-existed with Islam (Lovejoy 2004b:19).

Musical practice often exists within a socio-cultural context. It is necessary to uncover the specific contexts of Afro-Asian music. Certain genres, such as the goma of the Afro-Indians, exist within a religious context. Others such as Manhas in Sri Lanka are not tied to any religious practices or beliefs, but are practiced as a form of entertainment and only found among people of African descent. The elders in the Afro-Sri Lankan community state that even when intermarriage dilutes their physiognomy—their characteristic curly hair, for example—it will be possible to mark out their descendants by the music and dance inherited from their African ancestors.

Music and dance are the best indicators of cultural origin. This is partly universal and particularly true for Africans. Since many Africans in Asia were the result of forced migrations, perhaps music provided a medium to communicate their nostalgia and relieve their sorrow. Afro-Asians have shown that cultural traditions of diasporic communities can be retained in music, song, and dance. Songs persist in social memory. Performing arts—music and dance—are orally transmitted within families and social groups. Music may be one of the most natural cultural traits which migrants carried with them. African music is rhythmic and its melody is often provided by the human voice. Many Africans migrated eastward because they were sold as slaves—and it is unlikely that they all carried their instruments with them. However, it is easy to reproduce rhythm on borrowed instruments or make-shift instruments. African migrants have continued their music and dance traditions in the host societies. Afro-Asian music also illustrates how Africans affected their host societies as cultural brokers.

Hemal Jayasuriya composed a poem (below) which encapsulates the African migrants' predicament:

Migrants

Not of their own accord
They boarded ships, to sail
To them, still unknown lands
Lying in wait
For them, across the Indian Ocean
They went, then
From their here and now: Africa
To there: some lands in Asia
Becoming required cogs
In service wheels
A part of the whole
Making those lands move
To different rhythms
Drummed by many an other.

CHAPTER 6

The History and Sociology of African Migrants

As an important aspect of the past of both continents, the African presence in Asia is self evident. It also involves a third continent, Europe. This book has mapped out a sustained, long-distance yet under-recognized migration. The international academic community has overlooked the Indian Ocean migration until a few decades ago. Policymakers, welfare organizations, and human rights groups now realize that Afro-Asians should be included on their agendas.

I was invited by UNESCO to present a paper in Paris on "African Migration across the Indian Ocean" at a conference organized to "Commemorate the Struggle against Slavery and its Abolition." The paper was subsequently published in the *International Social Sciences Journal* (2006) and will be translated into English, French, Spanish, Russian, Arabic, and Chinese. Thereby it will reach a wide readership. The reactions that I continue to receive from various parts of the world are most encouraging.

Dr John Dayal (2007), a member of the National Integration Council, Government of India; National President, All India Catholic Union; Secretary General, All India Christian Council; and the President, United Christian Action, Delhi, states:

I read your article, "Trading on a Thalassic Network," in the Slavery special issue 188 June of the International Social Sciences Journal. It was terrific, an eye-opener. I am surprised that India has had no activity, not even by Human Rights groups, to mark the abolition of slavery day.... I am sure this will end up in a seminar or function in the coming months.

In China, Li Cunna (2007), who is translating my paper into Chinese, states:

I am reading your paper about African migrations across the Indian Ocean. I am very interested in it, for I have found little such study carried out in China. Your work is very meaningful for us to discover the real history of a part of the world.

Migrants in New Spaces

The movement of Africans to the East is rarely on the agendas at international conferences. One reason for this could be that it is difficult to detect the African presence in Asia. On the one hand, this reflects a long-standing process of assimilation, and on the other, a parallel tension concerned with marginalization. Assimilation is the process by which a minority gradually adopts the customs and attitudes of the prevailing culture. The term, which generally refers to a group process, evolved in anthropology. Nevertheless, it can also be examined on an individual level. It describes a change in an individual or group identity that results from continuous social interaction between a member or members of two groups such that one of the members enters into the other group. Assimilation is a one-way process—the outsiders relinquish their own culture for that of the dominant culture. Integration, on the other hand, is the process by which different groups have closer social, economic, and political relationships, while maintaining their own identities.

Anthropological accounts have perhaps placed more emphasis on the Afro-Asians living on the periphery. It surprises most people that some of Asia's African slaves were able to rise to positions of power through their loyalty and military capabilities. Some of the African slaves advanced themselves economically, gaining social prestige in the process.

Social mobility was possible through military skills and strength, either as an owned or freed slave. In Islamic India, some Africans rose to prominent military positions; in fact, the descendants of the royal Africans of Sachin and Janjira remind us of the glories that once made them conspicuous.

Lovejoy (2004b:7) states that race was the determinant of social relationships in the Americas. Nevertheless, economic mobility in parts of the Atlantic world enabled descendants of slaves to build social networks that cut across racial boundaries, even though this may only happen after several generations have been born in the host country. Sports and music are areas in which new migrants can make an impact on the host society or find a way to connect to the host society. This has been proven by the highly successful men and women of African origin in the fields of music and sport in the Americas and Europe.

Occasional traveler's accounts provide some details on the nature and conditions of the work of Africans in Asia. During the mid-nineteenth century, in the Sindh (Pakistan), African slaves were horse-keepers, grasscutters, day laborers, and apprentices in trades such as carpentry and blacksmithing (Burton 1992:254). They were paid allowances for food and clothing, but rarely allowed to eat with their masters. Being trusted servants of the prince, they rose to positions of authority. For example, Sidi Gosh Mohammed, an African, was the favorite attendant of the Ameer Sher Mohammed in the Sindh (Burton 1992:254).

Managing farflung empires demanded manpower, and capable and loyal militia. The slave trade offered a convenient supply of Africans who were able to fill these positions. Africans served all the European colonizers, excelling not only as soldiers but also as sailors, musicians, water carriers, interpreters, nannies, bodyguards, palanquin carriers, and divers in pearl fisheries.

Territorial invasion and defense of acquired land required an efficient military force and Africans filled this niche. Both Europeans and Asian rulers sought African soldiers. Muslim, Hindu, and Buddhist kings and leaders employed African mercenaries who were crucial to their military strength and their victories in wars. When political scenarios changed, however, Africans found themselves serving masters with different religious affinities. At other times, they were unfortunately out of military jobs.

Some Afro-Asians have had no access to social mobility and thus are marginalized in contemporary societies. However, through an Afro-Indian saint, Bava Gor (an Indian version of Baba Ghaur), some Afro-Indians have become mediators between the Saint and Indians of various religious beliefs who reach out for his powers. Afro-Gujaratis believe that their ancestor was an Abyssinian named Sidi Mubarak Nobi ("the blessed saint from Nubia"), who arrived in the thirteenth century. He became known as Bava Gor or Gori Pir and is believed to have developed the agate trade by enhancing its marketability; he also traded with Africa, the Persian Gulf, and the Middle East. He is believed to have traveled to Mecca and southern Iraq where he studied with Rifa'i Sufis whose leader gave him the honorific title, Baba Ghaur, which means "revered master of deep meditation" in Arabic.

Kamar Badshah, an Afro-Gujarati elder, believed that they should be receiving royalties for the agate that had been taken away by others. Moreover, he thought that the government should give them the rights to the agate fields (Catlin-Jairazbhoy and Alpers 2004:7). The land rights of voiceless Afro-Asians, not just in Gujarat but elsewhere too, need to be considered.

Afro-Gujaratis have found roles in Indian society as *fakirs* or Sufi mendicants. The shrines of Bava Gor are visited, not only by the Muslims but also by Zoroasthrians, Christians, and Hindus. According to Basu (1993:293), assimilation of the Afro-Gujaratis into the local society was brought about by their role as fakirs. Basu further asserts that slaves, who found themselves in Hindu India without a caste or ancestry, were transformed into a caste of black people through their role as fakirs. Fictive kinship ties were necessary for Afro-Gujaratis to assert marital relationships. These saints are believed to heal impotency and mental illness, and they attract many Indians reaching out to be blessed by the one who could cure their illnesses and deficiencies.

Basu (1993:293) reports on a slave's son in Surat, giving an idea of how slaves were brought from Zanzibar to Bombay. It also illustrates how the Bava Gor shrines can be places of communal interactions where

Afro-Indians not only get spiritual strength but form bonds with fellow Africans:

> My father was still a boy. One day he was playing with his younger sister on the beach in Zanzibar. Suddenly they were seized by a man and taken to a ship. Many Siddi were already there and they were all kept for many months. They arrived in Bombay. My father's sister died shortly after their arrival, but my father came to a sheth and he ran away. He heard the name of Bava Gor and found his way to his shrine. Here he met my nana (MF) and later married my mother.

Shroff (2007:311) mentions Asoo Appa, an Afro-Indian who is the caretaker of a Bava Gor shrine (*dargah*) in Mumbai (Bombay). Asoo Appa's grandfather served in the army of the Nizam of Hyderabad (Andhra Pradesh). The Asafiya dynasty of Hyderabad, which was established in 1724, had a royal guard of African slave-soldiers who also entertained their masters with African songs and dance. Several generations of Africans had lived in Hyderabad, and Asoo Appa's family had been in India for over a century. Once the nizam died, Asoo Appa's grandfather had relocated to Surat (north India) and later to Ahmedabad (north India). Asoo Appa was born in Ahmedabad. Her father, Abdul Rasak Sidi Bilal, was a singer of devotional songs—*qawal* (Arabic)—but she moved to Mumbai after her marriage. Her husband's family came to Mumbai from Jamnagar (in Gujarat). He had been the caretaker of a Bava Gor dargah in Jamnagar and had moved to Mumbai to perform the same task. When her husband married another woman and moved to a different part of Mumbai, Asoo Appa became the caretaker of the dargah.

In some cases, however, migrants, who share a common religion with people in the host country, are unable to integrate. The West African migrants who have lived in Israel since the 1980s were Christians. They did not feel comfortable attending the churches of the Arab Christians in Israel, partly due to their association of Arabs with Islam. Therefore, they established their own churches—African Initiated Churches—which catered to their religious needs and their cultural, social, and economic requirements.

Migration, whether voluntary or forced, has resulted in people coming across those of other faiths, particularly when placed in an alien cultural group. If we recognize that religious freedom is a fundamental human right, then most slaves were denied this right because they were not free to retain their religion. Many were converted. On the other hand, it could be argued that conversion has made it easier for migrants to assimilate to the host countries. In Islamic societies, conversion makes the outsider an insider. In a Christian milieu, converted slaves fitted in with the European colonizers. Those who converted became absorbed more easily. The difference in the two scenarios is that most of those who converted to Islam live in Islamic societies. The Christian convertees have become minorities in postcolonial nations.

Slaves used possession ceremonies as a form of both mimicking and coping with their enslavement (Khalifa 2006b:43). The zar ceremonies provided the enslaved and marginalized Africans with an opportunity for self-expression (Khalifa 2006b:60). According to Hunwick (2004:149), in the Mediterranean diaspora, African religious backgrounds provided mechanisms through which Africans coped with the psychological trauma brought about by enslavement, transportation, and transplantation into alien cultural environments. The slaves accustomed themselves to their new cultural milieu, displaying differing degrees of Islamization and naturalization. Enslaved Africans who migrated to Asia may have experienced similar traumas.

Intermarriage and Identity

In Muslim societies, Africans were absorbed into the kin system and this partially accounts for their invisibility. The status of concubines in Islam affected the process of assimilating for Africans, particularly in the East. The children of African concubines were free and this hastened their social mobility. For the concubines of the Christians, however, the status of their illegitimate children was decided by their owners.

People who are scattered or dispersed from their place of origin are called diasporans. Such people generally consider themselves to be of a common ancestral origin either ethnically or geographically. Diasporic identities connect migrants to a particular territory or homeland with which they identify or have a sense of belonging. Although they remain aware of their common ethnic ancestry, Afro-Asians now consider themselves Asian. After all, these Africans were born in Asia, and most have never been to Africa.

Since migration took place several generations ago, contemporary Afro-Asians no longer have any family ties in Africa. The long distances between Africa and the Asian countries in which migrants found themselves as well as their low economic status hindered them from even contemplating a return to their native lands in Africa. In most cases, they did not have the choice to return. Even if they ran away, they would not be able to make it back to Africa.

The application of the term *diaspora* to today's Afro-Asians has been contested by some academics. One may ask, how many generations does it take for a migrant group to become indigenous? While on-going debate on the most appropriate term to describe settler migrants continues, Afro-Asian communities receive little attention from academics, social workers, and policymakers. Asian countries have become homes to African migrants—and in most cases, the migrants do not have another home. Since several generations of their ancestors were also born in Asia, they are now indigenized. Yet, their African physiognomical features distinguish them from other Indians; however, sometimes the distinction is quite unclear. Often, curly hair is associated with negritude, both by other Asians and the Afro-Asians themselves.

The concept of the African diaspora is based on a triadic relationship: an African Homeland, Africans and their descendants, and an Adopted Residence or Home Abroad (Harris 2003). Although migrant Africans have adopted Asian countries as their Home, they are generally aware of their ethnic origins. Oral histories substantiate retentions of African languages, religious beliefs and practices, and musical expressions and dance forms, which rekindle memories and myths about the ancestral African Homeland. While Afro-Americans look to Africa as a Homeland, this is generally not the case with Afro-Asians, highlighting the extent to which Africans have been assimilated into Asian society. It is significant that the increased interest in transatlantic slavery and the plight of Afro-Americans encouraged the recognition of eastward-bound Africans. But for them, it is doubtful whether international attention would have fallen on Afro-Asians. The UNESCO Slave Route Project has been concentrating on the Atlantic for several years—and it is only beginning to turn its attention to the Indian Ocean.

When I lived in Nigeria, I came across African Americans who had come in search of their roots. They also wanted to help their African brothers and sisters with their expertise. My neighbor, Orville Johnson, an African-American choreographer, who lectured at the Department of Theatre Arts, University of Calabar, developed dance routines for Nigerians. He allowed members of his dance troupe to live in his large, modern, well-equipped flat and servant quarters which were situated nearby. I remember the rehearsals in Orville's living room when I casually dropped in on him. Sadly, African Americans realized that they had moved away culturally from their African kinfolk and they felt like outsiders. This is significant because it shows that cultural identity is separate from and beyond race.

Ethnicity and identity are sensitive political issues. In some parts of Asia, the current political climate does not allow migrants the freedom of expression. Even in liberty, there is no complete freedom. Ethnification, a process in which belonging is instrumental in getting access to political power, is not prevalent among Afro-Asians. Beckerleg (2007:290) conducted fieldwork among Palestinians of African origin and discovered that they lacked a common ethnicity. The principal distinction is between Arab and Jew in Palestine. Some Africans in Jerusalem have roots in Senegal while others originated from Nigeria, Chad, and Sudan—they were free migrants who came to Palestine as Muslim pilgrims during the nineteenth and twentieth centuries. Others had been slaves of Palestinian Bedouin who had stayed in the Negev after Israel was created in 1948.

In addition, Beckerleg (2007) included the Negev Bedouin who had become refugees in Gaza. Whether some Bedouin know the exact place in Africa that their ancestors had originated from is not clear. A Bedouin woman stated, "We just say Sudan because we do not know and because the name means place of black people. It could just as easily have been Congo!" (Beckerleg 2007:294). Most Bedouin, however, would say that they came from Sudan or Ethiopia. According to Israeli policy, the Bedouin of the Negev are not considered Arabs or permitted to serve in the army. Non-Bedouin Palestinians are called Arabs. Intermarriage occurred between Palestinians of African descent and Arabs. The paternal line determines the child's ethnicity. In this case, skin color is not relevant. For instance, a boy who is born white because his mother is white is still considered black if his father is black (Beckerleg 2007:298). Palestinians call black people *abed*, which means "slave" in Arabic, a word which stems from associating Africans with slavery.

Marriage and family life are important factors. It is interesting that the Ethiopian sailors who served on the ships of Portuguese and others in the sixteenth century took their wives and children with them (Linschoten 1855:267). The importance of marriage varies in different cultures and societies. Yet, it remains the key to the most basic of social institutions, the family, which is the main unit of socialization and economic cooperation. Some argue that marriage is essentially an economic partnership. It defines the social identity of the offspring and establishes bonds. In its many manifestations, marriage is a basic form of alliance in any society. Several factors led to intermarriage and miscegenation between Africans and Asians. Concubinage was widespread. Interracial relationships, whether driven by sociological or demographical reasons, occurred.

With the many generations of Africans born in India, most Afro-Indians now consider themselves as Indians. Many Africans remained isolated for several centuries, and endogamy was practiced among them. Therefore, they can be physically differentiated from other Indians, mainly by their curly hair and not necessarily by skin color. Some possess physiognomical features which are similar to those of the Africans. They are aware of their African roots. No doubt, belonging to two continents and two cultures creates a tension and affects how Afro-Indians construct their identities.

Some slaves, who were caught on slaving vessels by the British Royal Navy, were freed and sent to Bombay, Surat, Aden, Seychelles, or Mauritius. Forced migrants did not generally return to Africa; it was a one-way journey to Asia. The few freed Africans who were sent to Mauritius, Seychelles, and Kenya were exceptions. Some Africans in Bombay (or Mumbai Africans, as we would call them today) were sent to Kenya. They converted to Christianity, and when they settled in Freretown (near Mombasa), they remained apart, as the local Kenyans and other Africans there were Muslims. We know that some transatlantic African slaves lived with the hope that they would see their parents, relatives, and friends again, perhaps expecting to be ransomed when their whereabouts became known to their folk.

Only a few Ethiopian women were brought to the Deccan; this inevitably resulted in exogamy, gradually reducing the number of Habshis in the Deccan. The descendants of the African dynasties in Sachin and Janjira identify with the Muslim elite in India. Africans exported to Daman (Gujarat) were en route to Goa. Some were assimilated locally. Those who were sent to Diu (Gujarat) moved to Kathiawar (northwestern India), where there was a small demand for them until the nineteenth century. Then, a market for slaves developed in Kutch and possibly at Sindh, according to Machado (2004:19). This movement of slaves within India has diluted their presence as well as their strength today. As powerless minorities, they may be encouraged to assimilate. On the other hand, assimilation depends on the host societies and whether they would discriminate on the basis of race or would be open and accept them.

About twenty-five years ago, researchers at the Indian Statistical Institute in Kolkata (Calcutta) published an article on parental consanguinity of the Afro-Indians in Karnataka (Vijayakumar and Malhotra 1983). In 1981, they gathered their sample from the North Kanara district (western Karnataka) which included three religious groups— Hindu, Muslim, and Christian. The majority were Christians (156 couples), followed by Muslims (65 couples), and then Hindus (47 couples). This represented the distribution of Afro-Indians in the area—2,250 Christians, 1,750 Hindus, and 1,000 Muslims. The researchers discovered that matrilateral cross-cousin and uncle-niece marriages prevailed in all groups. In addition, the Muslims practised patrilateral parallel-cousin marriages. This was uncommon among the Christians, and there was only one such marriage among the Hindus. The most common form (67.86%) of marriage among all groups was matrilateral cross-cousin marriages. The Hindus had 12.76% of uncle-niece and aunt-nephew marriages. Out of 156 Christian couples, eighteen had unrelated marriages. Among the forty-seven Hindu couples, thirty-one had unrelated marriages. Of the sixty-five Muslim couples, thirty-five were unrelated. The rate of endogamy among the Muslims in this sample was higher than in other Muslim groups which had 27.63% consanguineous marriages. The percentage for the Hindu Afro-Indians (34.04%) was predictable, as the average figure was 30.33% for other Hindus of Karnataka. (No data was available for the other Christians in the state.)

According to Drewal (2004:146), Afro-Indians are "inside-outsiders" who have lived in India since medieval times. At various times, they had taken the side of Indians against Turks and Persians, in addition to marrying indigenous Indians. Drewal therefore considers Afro-Indians to be simultaneously and ambiguously both inside and outside the race and caste classification systems of identity. Most Afro-Indians came to Karnataka from the neighboring State of Goa. Some have been forced to leave agricultural work and take up other employment in the cities now, due to economic pressure and the change in labor markets. This is a global phenomenon—people are flocking to big cities in search of employment. The older generations are illiterate, but the younger ones attend school and a few have even entered higher education institutions. This is an achievement for this community that is marginalized. According to the 2001 Census of India, the literacy rate of Karnataka State was 67.04%. Since 1991, Karnataka has increased its literacy rate by 11%.

The Muslim Afro-Indians in Karnataka are Sunnis of the Hanafi School. In fact, they, prefer to be called muslims, although this is not an ethnic label. This is of interest, as it indicates their sense of belonging to the larger Islamic world. There are also Hindu Afro-Indians. Most of them converted through free will when they married Hindu women.

Afro-Indians appear to believe in spirits, charms, sacrifices, and ghosts. However, these beliefs are not unique to Africans, and unless we can ascertain that they are exclusive to Afro-Indians and not practised by other Indians, we cannot confirm that they are remnants of African culture. Trance or spirit possession ceremonies are found in South Asia among other religious groups.

However, Afro-Indians are not a cohesive group. Despite their common physiognomical features, they are divided by religious differences even within the same state. The Christian Afro-Indians are also divided—not all of them are Catholics, and some are Protestants. Recently, there has been a change of tact in trying to arouse cultural and historical consciousness in Afro-Indians at Karnataka. The Jesuit priests have decided to concentrate on cultural expressions in order to create an awareness of history and common ancestry, hoping that the Indians at large would feel the African presence. Educating a minority has its demands, but it is even more taxing to focus the attention of the majority on the subaltern. In this wake, a *Kala and Sanskriti Workshop* (Arts and Culture Workshop) was organized in Karnataka. By the mid-1990s, an Afro-Indian performance troupe was established by the Siddi Development Society of Yellapur, Karnataka. Eric Ozario, a Konkani cultural-activist from Mangalore, led the workshop. Five elders and twenty-five young Afro-Indians were invited to participate in the workshop which involved the Afro-Indians learning Konkani and Hindu songs, in addition to their own traditional songs.

These Afro-Indians wanted to preserve their language and way of life. They have a clear vision of the future. A Muslim Afro-Indian had wanted to start an exchange programme in Nigeria so that he could learn the Yoruba language and in turn teach Nigerians his Afro-Indian language. Another wanted to establish a cultural center. Producing a CD of their music and distributing it throughout the world were the aspirations of another Afro-Indian. Others wanted to join a music group and tour India to educate Indians about their culture. They know how they could achieve their goals—attending school, studying their language and history, forming cultural groups, and contacting record companies. A tension exists between keeping their own identity and becoming part of the social and economic systems of India. Their objective is to develop a sense of their own identity through the strengthening and showcasing of their linguistic and cultural heritage—and becoming educators of the Indian public at large. They display impressive ambitions. No doubt, the young Afro-Indians wish to examine their cultural roots and strengthen them. Drewal (2004) draws attention to the Yoruba proverb, "A river that forgets its source, dries up," which is appropriate for all migrants, not only Africans.

It is difficult to know how typical the Karnataka Afro-Indian group is without comparative data on other communities. Their aspirations serve as a model for others as well as dispersed peoples throughout the world. While academic debates are concentrating on the desire, or the lack thereof, to return to the original homeland, Afro-Indians have demonstrated that migrants want to recreate a home outside home, even after many generations of indigenization. This brings to the fore important issues about migrants, especially, their awareness of ethnic origins and cultural expressions in creating a new identity. One might expect that the impoverished status of these Afro-Indians would force them to lose their "outsider" label and aspire to become assimilated. They are not driven by the laws of economics, but by their emotions and consciousness. Even though they generally say that they are Indians, which they are now, there is a tenuous link with Africa and African culture that they have yet to experience first hand. It is difficult to articulate the emotion that Afro-Asians express when they see an African. It is lodged deeply in them. As outsiders, we are unable to feel the emotional link. The Afro-Indian (Siddi) leader of the Siddi Development Project (SDP) in Uttara Kannada, Karnataka, wrote a letter to Nelson Mandela. He received an acknowledgement from Mandela's Office. His reactions demonstrate what Afro-Indians feel about Africa and Africans (see below).

> You cannot imagine how happy I and my fellow-Siddis were when we received this letter. Look, this was the first time we Siddis contacted another African in Africa and the President came to know about our existence. By now he has forgotten about us but at least it is registered in his office that we Siddis in India exist and that we contacted him. This is a very precious letter for us and we have kept it in a safe place. Actually, I came to know about President Nelson Mandela only after I saw a photograph of him shaking hands with

the President of India. I didn't know who he was but realised that he must be an important person as he is shaking hand with the President of India. I thought for myself "who is this Siddi"? When I enquired with a long hair friend of mine [a phrase the Siddis use to describe a person who is not a Siddi] he told me about President Mandela's visit. Then I came to know that he is the President of Africa [sic]. So, I discussed with other Siddi leaders and we decided to go to Delhi and meet him in person and tell him about us. But then it was too late, he had already returned to Africa [sic], so that's why we wrote to him. Anyhow, if he comes again to India we will definitely try to meet him. (Camara 2004:110)

Many Afro-Indians are hidden away in forest villages of the Western Ghats. There is little public awareness of their presence. A few know that the Sports Authority of India's Gandhinagar Center in Gujarat actively sought Afro-Gujaratis around the Gir Forest in Saurashtra and tried to develop their athletic potential and talents. They hoped that these athletes would excel at national events and more importantly at the Olympic games, and win medals for India. This plan was effected in 1987 at Karnataka. Gujarat followed the next year (Micklem 2001:38). Nevertheless, the scheme failed due to the number of dropouts. The Afro-Gujaratis had been offered handsome job packages by Indian companies, and the short-term financial gains and immediacy of those jobs were more attractive to them than the long hours of training required to attain the high standards necessary for excelling at international competitions. The experiment was a failure, but there is no reason why it could not be revived with added incentives and psychological training to enhance the will power to continue to stay in the camps. Ahmed Vali Makwana, a leader from the Afro-Gujarati community, requested a small sports center nearer to their homes, as it would provide the necessary conditions for them to train. The emphasis on athletics can stereotype Afro-Indians and unintentionally send negative signals about them. On the other hand, it might bring awareness to their physical strength, courage, and dedication, all of which are encapsulated in their glorious past within parts of India, as military commanders and leaders.

Minda (2007) draws attention to the changing identities of the Afro-Hyderabadis in Andhra Pradesh. Identities are not static and they change depending on the pressures placed upon them. Most Afro-Hyderabadis are Muslims, but some of them are Christians too. In the past, cross-religious marriages among Chaush occurred, however, they have been replaced with interracial marriages between Christian Indians and Christian Chaushs. This new development is significant and no doubt reflects the religious fervor in India at present. It also illustrates that racial difference is not an issue in India and has been over-ridden by other factors that are currently in vogue. As a result, Christian Chaushs are assimilating faster than their Muslim counterparts. On the other hand, given that Christianity is associated with the West, Christian Chaushs aspire to emigrate to Anglo-Saxon countries: U.K., U.S.A,, Australia, and New Zealand. On the other hand, the Muslim Chaushs generally in-marry and two families can be related through the marriages of several members. This is biologically not conducive, as it carries the risk of increasing hereditary diseases and weakens the progeny.

Muslim Chaushs identify with the Arabs. This is not surprising because some of them came to India through Islamic countries: Saudi Arabia, Yemen, Bahrain, Oman, Iraq, Pakistan, Zanzibar and Somalia. They spoke Arabic and were acculturated, thereby concealing their African roots. While their exact African origins are unknown to most Chaushs, those who came from Somalia know their tribes and genealogies. Abdullah bin Mohammad recalled his male ancestors from several generations: Abdullah bin Mohammad bin Hassan bin Farah bin Ismail bin Abdullah bin Osman bin Shire bin Shirdon bin Abane bin Burare (Minda 2007:332). He belonged to the Haberyenus clan. His memory was impressive. Like most Afro-Asian communities today, Afro-Hyderabadis have a mixed ancestry. While some are recent migrants who know their clan names, others have an older history that is connected to the slave trade on which most of the details have been lost. Second generation immigrants were told where they originated by their fathers.

India's colonization added new ethnic groups to the subcontinent. The descendants of the Portuguese and British are now called Anglo-Indians because the Luso-Indians have become subsumed within the later group of mixed European descendants. The offspring from British or Portuguese and African unions are also included in this category. This adds another facet to the effects of colonization—people who descended from the colonizer have been simply left behind in postcolonial nations. Not belonging to the indigenous peoples, the Anglo-Indians, Anglo-Africans, and Luso-Africans became misfits due to the changes in political power and the newly important social values. Having been westernized, they speak English as well as the local Indian language. They are Christians. These are not attributes which were valued in a postindependent climate, especially shortly after decolonization.

The Chaushs are now caught in the poverty trap. Since they do not use birth control methods, they have several children who they cannot afford to send to school. Formal education for girls ends when they reach puberty; as a result, they only look forward to marriage and then motherhood. It is even often impossible for the boys to further their education, as they are forced to find paid employment.

Most Chaushs are unwilling to leave their homes or familiar surroundings to take up jobs elsewhere. Some are drawn by the economic differences and the labor demand in the Middle East. Returning home once a year to visit the family, friends and more importantly, the surroundings that renew and strengthen their communal identity is an established pattern. As Muslims, they fit well into Arab countries, but identity is, of course, beyond religion. The Chaushs, who have had to move out of African cavalry guards to nearby places—Chintal Basti, Veer Neger, and Irru Mansil—due to space constraints, visit their "headquarters" regularly. This shows how people can get attached to their environment; it also illustrates what agony people experience when they are suddenly uprooted and taken away to faraway lands.

In neighboring Sri Lanka, Bertolacci (1817) observed that a new race was emerging due to the intermarriages between Kaffir soldiers and Sri Lankan women. He noted that this new progeny was insufficient in maintaining the existing levels of soldiers in the local regiments. He also commented that the Kaffir soldiers, who came from Mozambique and other countries on the African coasts as well as Madagascar, served in the colonial regiments. In the early twentieth century, Elsie Cook, a British educational consultant, describing the Puttalama district stated that "there are also remnants of foreign regiments who were stationed in this district and married and settled in the island, notably a *Kaffir* element from South Africa" (Cook 1953:330). She added that a Kaffir regiment, which was stationed in Puttalama district (northwestern province) during the nineteenth century, intermarried with the Sinhalese; it is no doubt the reason why some Sri Lankans have "black skin and woolly hair, more like inhabitants of Africa" (Cook 1953:272). This is of interest, considering that not many South Africans seemed to have come to Asia. Further research is necessary to ascertain if they came under different circumstances and whether their history has been subsumed by the focus on the slave trade. Africans in Asia lost their status, as their once sought-after military skills were suddenly not needed. After the Kandyan kingdom was seized by the British, and the island's administration unified under British rule in 1815, there was little demand for good soldiers and it was costly to maintain idle soldiers. The British dismantled the garrison in the northwestern part of the island and retired the soldiers, giving them land. However, the Afro-Sri Lankans did not adjust well to this new way of life. They have been unable to enroll in the Sri Lankan universities so far, despite the availability of subsidised education up to the tertiary level. The government's encouragement of education and literacy has had an effect on interethnic relationships; children of different ethnic groups study together in the same classrooms, and there is no segregation of races. This affects the choice of partners. In Sri Lanka, therefore, free education has accelerated intermarriage among the descendants who are living on the periphery of society. Descendants of slaves and other ethnic groups studying together in the same classroom help breakdown the social compartmentalization that could otherwise exist.

Historical literature on the African presence in India assumes that Africans are completely separated and isolated from the host societies, or that they are in the process of assimilating which would ultimately erase their "African-ness" (Basu 2003:223–224). The reality may be somewhere in between, but further research is needed in order to ascertain the current situation.

Some migrants who are part of a global network are connected through trade. For forced migrants who have been working under conditions that violate human rights and have been mostly marginalized, there are no such networks. Today, Afro-Asians are dispersed throughout various countries.

Jayanti Patel, President of the Indian Radical Humanist Association, draws attention to the current plight of most Afro-Indians who, according to him, live in a caste-conscious and hierarchical society. He thinks that it is very difficult to acquire upward mobility and human dignity in such a sociocultural structure and milieu (Patel 2004:214). Africans were being placed not only within Islamic settings in India but also in Hindu areas. In Hindu India, Africans fall outside the kinship systems; they are outside the caste system. Yet, in Muslim India, Africans became absorbed into the kin system. The dynasties of Sachin and Janjira, which lasted until the mid-twentieth century, were composed of Africans who were brought to India as slaves and later became commanders and leaders in the Islamic setting.

Some Afro-Indians have been classified as tribals, while others are considered Scheduled Tribes or Scheduled Castes. Afro-Indians in Saurashtra (Gujarat) and Uttara Kannada (Karnataka), receive benefits as Scheduled Tribes. The former group receives less funding from central government and thus obviously discontented with the different classifications for the same ethnic group. Educated Afro-Indians recognize their power in collective bargaining—and they are anxious to form an All India Association. At the moment, however, this remains an unfulfilled dream.

In Indonesia, the Ghanaian recruits were males, and through intermarriage with local women, they appear to have accelerated the process of assimilation. Moreover, the Ghanaians were treated as part of the European community by the Indonesians, despite obvious physiognomical differences. This raises the question of identity. The Ghanaians were called *Londo Ireng* in Javanese and *Belanda Hitam* in Malay, meaning "Black Dutchman" or "Black White Man" (Van Kessel 2007:249). This terminology reflects how Indonesians viewed the Ghanaians—though black in skin color, they were white in other aspects.

In the 1930s, black soldiers from Surinam (Dutch Guyana) volunteered and served in the Dutch East Indian army. They were included with the Afro-Indonesians and may have had Ghanaian roots. The offspring of Indonesian and Ghanaian unions, Afro-Indonesians, were known to be loyal to the Dutch cause and identified with the colonial regime. Therefore, in 1945, they were viewed with hostility by Indonesian nationalists. Although Afro-Indonesians had family ties in Indonesia, it was not safe for them to remain there under the circumstances. The British evacuated the Euro-Indonesians and the Afro-Indonesians to safe places such as Siam (today's Thailand) (Van Kessel 2007:264). Once power was transferred to the Indonesians in 1949, the Dutch army repatriated.

Several Afro-Indonesians opted to stay where they were born. While some kept Dutch nationality, others accepted Indonesian citizenship. The status quo changed again, especially for some Afro-Indonesians who felt that independent Indonesia was unable to offer their families future opportunities. Van Kessel (2007:265) reports that Daan Cordus held a good position in Jakarta with a Dutch shipping company but sailed to the Netherlands in 1954, together with his family—mother, wife, three daughters, two sisters and two brothers. Interestingly, the Dutch were less concerned about their race or origins than their religion. They had been Catholics and settled in Eysden, a rural town in southern Netherlands. The Dutch did not convert the Muslim Ghanaians who they enlisted in their army. However, the children of these soldiers, who were originally born in Indonesia, were baptized as Christians, mostly Catholics (Van Kessel 2007:254). The Afro-Indonesians were treated like the Euro-Indonesians in the Netherlands. There were about 300,000 evacuees from Indonesia during the first decade after World War II (Van Kessel 2007:265). Indeed, the physiognomical distinction between an Afro-Indonesian and Euro-Indonesian was often blurred. When the Indonesian-Africans grew older, they had reunions and their hybrid identity was apparent in the atmosphere of their get-togethers. Indonesian food, Javanese dances, African music, and Ghanaian fashion shows abounded on these occasions (Van Kessel 2007).

Language and Indigenization

Language is a key factor in indigenization and assimilation as well. Outsiders who learn the local tongues are able to fit into the new host societies more quickly than are others. Some Afro-Asians, inevitably, spoke a western language, due to the day-to-day demands of communication. European expansion brought together voyagers, merchants, missionaries, and settlers with Africans and Asians speaking a myriad of languages. As a result, Europeans had to employ a variety of methods to communicate. They took interpreters on their ships whenever possible. At other times, they relied on the availability of bilingual and multilingual peoples in their ports of call. While initial contacts could be established by offering diplomatic gifts and non-verbal communication, prolonged and sustained commercial exchanges required a verbal means of communication.

The Portuguese were the first Europeans to take Africans to Asia. They took shipments of captive Africans to the Persian Gulf, India, China, and Japan. Communication was an essential and powerful "instrument" in colonial rule. Africans acted as interpreters between the Portuguese and Asians. Peter Mundy, who was in Macau during the early seventeenth century, referred to Africans as "Negroes, Caphers, Eathiopian Abissin or Curled heads." On 18 July 1637, Mundy (1907:178) wrote, "And presently John Mounteney and Thomas Robinson went abourd the Admirall, the Cheife Mandreine, where were certaine Negroes, fugitives of the Portugalls, that interpreted between them."

Writing again in 1637, Mundy notes that "the aforesaid interpreter was a Chincheo, runaway from the Portugalls, att our being att Macao, wo spake a little bad language. There is another, named Antonio, a Capher Eathiopian Abissin or Curled head, that came to and froe about messages as interpreter, little better than the other runaway alsoe from the Portugalls to the Chinois" (Mundy 1907:192). These examples illustrate that Africans had lived in Macau long enough to learn the local language, Cantonese. They would have been multilingual.

Cultural brokers were able to cross borders and connect local communities to larger regional or even international systems. They were part of the local, social, and economic networks. Crossing borders and communicating with others necessitated linguistic links. As brokers and people in between two cultures, Africans learned Asian languages, or the lingua franca of the area.

The multiethnic and multilingual situations that grew out of bringing together people of different ethnic backgrounds, who spoke several mother-tongues, have resulted in creole societies and creole languages. The word creole has several meanings in different academic disciplines. In 1712, the first Portuguese dictionary describes a *Crioulo* as "a slave born in his owner's house, like the chicken born at home, not bought outside." Contact languages—Pidgins and Creoles—evolve in situations where a medium of communication is necessary between people who do not speak each other's mother-tongue. A Creole is generally accepted as the mother-tongue of a community, unlike a Pidgin which is nobody's mother-tongue.

As they took orders from westerners, Africans learned to speak pidginized and creolized versions of European languages. Sometimes the creole language became a lingua franca and then Africans were in demand as interpreters. The Afro-Sri Lankans are an example. Africans were brought from Goa to Sri Lanka in the Portuguese Era (1505–1658). They spoke the Indo-Portuguese of Ceylon, which is related to other Indo-Portuguese dialects found in coastal India: Diu, Daman, Korlai, Negapatnam, Mangalore, Norte (Bombay, Bassein), and Cochin (de Silva Jayasuriya 1999b, 1999c, 1999d, 1999e, 2000a, 2000b, 2000c, 2001d, 2001e, 2002c, 2002d, 2004e). As the lingua franca during the entire Dutch Era (1658–1796) of Sri Lanka, Indo-Portuguese was the prestige language of the day. Even after the British took over from the Dutch, Afro-Sri Lankans continued to be mother-tongue speakers of the Indo-Portuguese of Ceylon. Only after independence and changes in education policy, affecting the medium of education and the introduction of indigenous languages, Sinhala and Tamil, did the Afro-Sri Lankans switch from Indo-Portuguese. Significantly, they did not switch from one prestige language to another. They speak Sinhala, the language of the majority of Sri Lankans, not English. A few of them also speak

Tamil, depending on whether they have lived in areas where Tamil is prevalent. This is probably a measure of the extent of indigenization.

A similar situation exists in India. In Karnataka, next to Goa, there are Afro-Indians who speak Kannada, the main language of the state, and Konkani, the language spoken in Goa and the Konkan coast. They also speak Urdu, Hindi, and some English, due to the English medium schools that are accessible to them in Bangalore, Mangalore, Pune, Mundgod, Haliyal, Yellapur, and Chennai (Madras) (Obeng 2007b:personal communication). It is significant to note that those studying in English are not all Christians. The Kannada medium schools are supported by the Karnataka government. The English medium schools are supported by various, mainly Christian sources—Seventh Day Adventist Church, Jesuits, Sisters of Holy Cross. The fee-charging schools are supported by parental income.

In Andhra Pradesh, where Afro-Indians called Chaushs were brought in as the nizam's guards, they spoke Urdu. They also spoke Telugu, the main language of the state.

In the northwestern state of Gujarat, Afro-Indians speak Gujarati, Urdu, and Hindi. A few can also speak English. Africans in Mumbai speak Marathi, Hindi or Gujarati if they have migrated from Gujarat (Shroff 2007). In addition the descendants of the African dynasties of Sachin and Janjira intermarry with the Indian Muslims belonging to the higher socioeconomic group. According to McLeod (2007:personal communication) who has been in touch with them while working on the book, *African Elites in India*, which he co-edited with Kenneth Robbins, the two elite families whom he knows in Janjira and Sachin speak English at home and even to each other. Being Muslims, they also know Urdu and can therefore speak in "bazaar Hindi" with their servants. Marathi and Konkani were languages that were spoken in Janjira. Although these languages are not spoken widely by the elite Africans now, some Marathi is spoken in Janjira. Jasdanwalla (2007:personal communication), a royal Afro-Indian, confirms this, but she also adds that her relatives can read Arabic due to their knowledge of Urdu.

The Afro-Sindhis are a group that should be studied for several reasons. Most importantly, some information on the language that they spoke among themselves during the mid-nineteenth century is available. Burton (1992:256), who served in the British army in the Sindh, left an ethnographic description of local life. He mentions that the Africans who were born in the Sindh only knew a few words of an African language, which they had learnt from their migrant parents. However, the Africans were able to speak in a language that the local Sindhis could not understand. Whenever they could not recall an African word, they had substituted a Sindhi word. This implies that they were bilingual by that time.

Bilinguals or multilinguals employ two strategies when speaking— code switching and code mixing. In the first instance, they switch from one language to the other, in the same utterance, while speaking in chunks of one language and then the other. By adopting the notations of Hamers and Blanc (1983), I have schematized the speech for a bilingual in Swahili and Sindhi. L means language, Sw means Swahili, and Si means Sindhi:

Code Switching: $L_{sw}/L_{si}/L_{sw}/L_{si}/etc$

In code mixing, the speaker would simply mix the two languages in an unprecedented and free manner. It can be schematized as below:

Code Mixing: $/L_{sw}/(L_{si}L_{sw})/L_{sw}/(L_{si}L_{sw})/L_{sw}/etc$

The Afro-Sindhis can recall some "African" words. Since Africans from several tribes came to Pakistan, Swahili would have bridged the inter-tribal linguistic gap. Africans who spoke several tribal languages as their mother-tongues would have learned Swahili by either spending some time in countries where it was widely spoken, or being exposed to it as a lingua franca in East Africa. The Swahili words that the Africans used in the Sindh fall into semantic categories relating to numbers, anatomy, clothes, food, transport, fauna, and flora. The Sidi words in the Sindh offer an insight into language contact and perserverance among migrants. Most borrowings are nouns but a few have been verbs as well. When one linguistic group introduces a new object or concept to another, a word is also borrowed along with the object. When diverse cultures come into contact, nouns are usually the first words to be borrowed. Not surprisingly, there are many nouns in Burton's list of "African words." In addition, there are a few verbs (*akanepá, akáje, kaletá, uje, usmáme*), an adjective (*gema*), pronouns (*miye, weye, yore,*) and a demonstrative (*hii*) in Burton's list.

Swahili means "coast." Its etymon is Arabic—*sāhil* (singular) and *swāhil* (plural) (Dalby 1970:286). The Swahili are a mixed community of Arabs and Africans that dates back to the seventh and eighth centuries. Due to wars in Arabia, they were forced to migrate and settle down in East Africa. The grammar of Swahili identifies it as a Bantu language. The fusion with Arabic went beyond language and spilled over to the cultures of the people bound by a common faith, Islam. Swahili was the language of the Zanj Empire, formed before 1000. By the twelfth century, Swahili had spread down the East African coast to the Zambesi River and Mozambique. Swahili colonies were also established in the Comoro Islands and the northwestern coast of Madagascar. As the Portuguese controlled most of this area during the sixteenth and seventeenth centuries, some Portuguese words have understandably entered Swahili (*bandera* from Portugese *bandeira* meaning "flag"). More importantly, Swahili was used in the British East African colonial army. Around 1800, Swahili-speaking traders went to the hinterland to capture slaves and get ivory. Thereafter, Swahili became the lingua franca in the Central African Lake District and the Congo.

Swahili belongs to the Sabaki group of Bantu languages spoken along the northeastern coast. There are about 200 million Swahili speakers altogether. Swahili is the national language of Tanzania and Kenya. It is also spoken in parts of Somalia, Uganda, Rwanda, Burundi, Zaire, Malawi, Zambia, the Democratic Republic of Congo, and Mozambique. It has been spoken since 800, when people from the Great Lakes area went to the coast. As the Swahili peoples were engaged in maritime trading, their language became established in the coastal settlements from Mogadishu in Somalia to Cape Delgado in Mozambique. Swahili was the outcome of the contact between Arabic-speaking traders and indigenous Bantu-speakers. Many Swahili converted to Islam which resulted in many Arabic words being borrowed by Swahili. Some Swahili words spoken by the Afro-Sindhis—*Barédi, Dámo, Falázi, Gamirah, Kofiah, Sahni, Samli, Zahabo*—have Arabic etyma. There are also borrowings from other languages in the list given below—for example, *nyembe* (from *amba* Gujarati) and *bunduki* (from Arbic, Turkish or Urdu). Several Swahili coastal cities became important centers of Indian Ocean commerce. When Zanzibar became the capital of the Omani Sultanate, the Swahili dialect of Kiunguja became prestigious. Swahili was used for colonial administration—and it was the language of interethnic communication as well.

Often, troops were identified by similarities in ethnicity and organized according to racial or geographical origin, indicating that tribal differences were irrelevant. Therefore, it is not surprising that Swahili would have served as the lingua franca of a multilingual population. It could also have become the language of interethnic communication and the language spoken between the master and slave, or commander and soldier in some instances. Although Swahili was the mother-tongue of some Africans, it was the lingua franca for others. In what follows, I have set out some "African" words that were spoken by the Afro-Sindhis. I have called this language Afro-Sindhi. Many words appear to have Swahili equivalents, and they have also been given below. In some instances, the meanings are different in Afro-Sindhi and Swahili, but that is expected. I used a Swahili-English dictionary (Johnson 1939) to check the words given below. I thank Dr. Jacky Maniacky (Africa Museum, Teruven, Belgium), who specializes in African Linguistics, for helping me identify the Swahili equivalents of some obscure words.

Afro-Sindhi Words	Meaning to Afro-Sindhis	Swahili Equivalent	Meaning in Swahili
Akábijá	sell	*bei*	(price)
Akáje	come	(v) *kuja*	come
Akanedá	go away	(v) *kwenda*	go away
Akanepá	give	(v) *kupa*	give
Akchukolá	carry away	(v) *kuchukua*	carry

Afro-Sindhi Words	Meaning to Afro-Sindhis	Swahili Equivalent	Meaning in Swahili
Akúnah	(there) is none	hakuna	there is/are no
Babayá	father	baba yangu	(my father)
Bandera	a kind of cap	bendera	flag
Bandúk	musket	bunduki	(gun)
		bunduki ya mrao	musket
Báredi	cold weather	baridi	cold (in the head)
Begá	shoulder	mbega/bega	shoulder
Búri	a hookah	buruma	hookah
Buzzi	a goat	mbuzi	goat
Chhiní	earth, flat ground	chini	on the ground
Chídore	a finger	kidole	finger
Chombo	a ship	chombo	ship
Dámo	blood	damu	blood
Devo	the beard	ndevu	beard
Dizzi	a plantain	ndisi	plantain
Druguángo	brother	ndugu yangu	(my brother)
		ndugu	brother
Dupuko	a mouse	puku	(field rat/mouse)
Fáká	a cat	paka	cat
Falási	a horse	farasi	horse
Fura	the nose	pua	nose
Gáo	a shield	ngao	shield
Gema	good	Njema	good, fine
Gerá/Gamirah	a camel	ngamia	camel
Gopingá	bent, crooked	(v) kupinda	bent, croomed
Guá	sugar cane	muwa	sugar cane
Gukú	a cock	kuku	hen
Gurúe	a pig	nguruwe	pig
Hi	this	hii	this
Juwa	the sun/a day	jua	sun
		siku	(a day)
Kaletá	come	(v) kuleta	(bring)

Afro-Sindhi Words	Meaning to Afro-Sindhis	Swahili Equivalent	Meaning in Swahili
Khánjo	a shirt	*kansu*	shirt
Khundoro	a sheep	*kondoo*	sheep
Kisimgurá	a hare	*sungura*	hare
Kisú	a knife	*kisu*	knife
Kofiah	a cap	*kofia*	cap
Kummi	ten	*kumi*	ten
Lumbuángo	a sister	*umbu wange*	my sister
Máchho	an eye	*macho*	eyes
Májí	water	*maji*	water
Mákomo	the hand	*mkono*	hand
Mámáyá	mother	*mama yangu*	my mother
Mánámukki	a woman	*mwanamke*	woman
Marimiya	my/mine	*mali yako*	my property
Mariyúre	his	*mali yule*	his/her property
Márome	a man	*mume*	(husband)
		mwanaume	(man)
Masekiro	the ear	*masikio*	(ears)
Máwe	a hill/a stone	*mawe*	stones
Mawingo	a cloud	*mawingu*	clouds
Mazewá	the breast	*masiwa*	milk
Menú	a tooth	*meno*	tooth
Mgongo	a back	*mgongo*	back
Misare	an arrow	*mishale*	(arrows)
Miye	I	*miye*	I
Mme	four	*nne*	four
Moesi	a moon/a month	*mwesi*	moon/month
Moto	fire	*moto*	fire
Moya	one	*moja*	one
Mromo	the mouth	*mdomo*	mouth
Msetemi	a jungle	*msituni*	(in the jungle)
Mtoto	a child	*motto*	child
Muani	eight	*themuni*	eighth part

Afro-Sindhi Words	Meaning to Afro-Sindhis	Swahili Equivalent	Meaning in Swahili
Muguru	a foot	mguu	foot
Mukátí	bread	mkate	bread
Mukokí	a spear	mkuki	spear
Mutámá	sorghum	mtama	sorghum
Mutomá	a slave	mtumwa	slave
Ngombe	a cow	ng'ombe	cattle/cow
Nkufá	a corpse	(v) kufa	(die)
Nyámmá	flesh	nyama	flesh/meat
Nyatí	a buffalo	nyati	buffalo
Nyembe	a mango	mwembe	mango tree
		embe	mango (fruit)
Nyoere	hair	nywele	hair
Nyumba	a house	nyumba	house
Okáre	sit	(v) kukaa	sit
Perhi	two	mbili	two
P'hani	sea	pwani	(beach)
P'hep'ho	cold	upepo	wind
Pinde	a bow	upindi	bow
Rupángá	a sword	upanga	sword
Sahabo	gold	dhahabu	gold
Sahni	a cup	sahani	cup (dish, plate)
Samorí	clarified butter	samli	butter
Sarawali	trousers	suruali	trousers
Sewa	a pigeon	njiwa	pigeon
Siko	night	siku	day
		usiku	night
Simbah	a lion	simba	lion
Singo	the neck/throat	shingo	neck
		koo	throat
Tahtu	three	tatu	three
Thano	five	tanu/tano	five
Thembre	an elephant	tembo	elephant

Afro-Sindhi Words	Meaning to Afro-Sindhis	Swahili Equivalent	Meaning in Swahili
Thende	dates	*tende*	date (fruit)
Uje	come	(v) *kuja*	come
Umbuá	a dog	*mbawa*	dog
Usmáme	stand	(v) *kusimama*	stand
Utanbo	stomach	*tumbo*	stomach
Vidorí	a finger	*vidole/kidole*	fingers/finger
Vurá	rain	*mvua*	rain
Wápi	where?	*Wapi*	where
Weye	thou	*weye/wewe*	you
Yure	he	*yule*	(Pronoun emphatic)

Sir Richard Burton wrote down these words as they were pronounced by one of the most intelligent Africans. He later consulted with other Afro-Sindhis to ensure their accuracy and meaning. Burton was not a linguist; he had no knowledge of African languages. He had not visited East Africa when he recorded these words. When words are adopted into another language, phonetic changes occur in order to suit the model of the mother-tongue speakers of the borrowing language. In addition, it is not surprising to find that the meaning of some words have changed from Swahili.

However, Burton did not name the "African language" spoken by the Afro-Sindhis. He confirms that two types of African slaves lived in the Sindh at that time—those born locally (*ghara-jao* meaning "serf born in the house") and those brought in from Muscat and other eastern Arabian coasts. The former category would have been bilingual, but the newly arrived Africans would have tried to speak in an "African language." The records of Richard Burton indicate that Sindhi Muslim men married *sidiyani* (female Africans) in the mid-nineteenth century. Their children were called *gaddo*, and the *quadroon* (a person with one African grandparent—a "quarter-blooded person") was called *kambrani* (Burton 1992).

Freeman-Grenville (1971:8-11) identifies nineteen "tribal names" given by Burton as places or tribes in Tanzania (given below), except for three names (*mukodongo, myasenda, temaluye*) that he is unable to identify. They appear in the *Handbook of Tanganyika* (Moffett 1958:171).

"Tribal Names"	Name in Tanganyika
Dengereko	Ndengereko
Dondere	Ndonde
Gindo	Ngindo
Kamang	Kamanga
Makonde	Makonde
Makua	Makua
Matumbi	Matumbi
Mkami	Mkami
Msagar	Msagara
Mudoe	Mdoe
Murima	Mrima
Murima-ph'ani	Mrima pwani
Muwhere	Mkwere
Myas	Mnyasa
Mzigra	Mzigua
Nizizima	Mzizima
Nyamuezi	Nyamwezi
Zalama	Zaramo
Zinzigari	Zanzibari

Lodhi (2000:40) draws attention to the contacts that took place on the East African coast between Bantu/Swahili language and the Cushitic, Arabic, Persian, Indian languages, and Indonesian. As a result, there are Arabic, Persian, Indic, Dravidian, Portuguese, and English borrowings in Swahili.

Sindhi, an Indic language, is spoken in the Sindh. Sir Bartle Frere, who was the Commissioner of the Sindh in 1851, decreed the compulsory use of Sindhi instead of Persian. After Indian independence and the partition of Pakistan from India in 1947, the Hindu Sindhis fled the province and crossed over to India.

In Pakistan, the Balochs of African descent have assimilated into the population at large. The language spoken is Urdu. Contact between the Makran and the African littoral (eastern and northeastern) continued until the first part of the twentieth century. As a result, elderly Baloch sailors are able to give first-hand accounts of these cross-continental experiences. Badalkhan (2006) mentions a sailor who stated that they learned the "language in Africa" (Swahili) and also songs. He spoke fluent Swahili; he also learned Arabic since he visited Middle Eastern ports regularly. They were given the necessary conditions to learn the local languages while they were stuck at ports in between monsoons.

Minda (2007:332) reports of an Afro-Hyderabadi, Feroz bin Abdullah, who recollects his father greeting his friends in Swahili. Memories of migrants have faded now because migration took place many centuries ago. Yet linguistic analyses of Afro-Asian songs in which are embedded some words from their ancestral languages could be performed.

Occasionally, there are records of slave names. The ancestors of some Maldivians were Africans. It is well known in oral history that five slaves—Sangoaru, Laalu, Marjan, Masud, and Muizz—were brought back by a Maldivian sultan returning from the Hajj. Today, Sangoaru's descendants are well integrated into the Maldivian sociopolitical structure. One of Sangoaru's grand-daughters married an Atoll chief, an important official who is in charge of the administrative affairs of an entire Atoll or group of islands. The Republic of Maldives consists of 1,190 islands that are geologically formed into Atolls, which are kind of clusters with a varied number of islands. However, for administrative convenience, the islands were grouped into Atolls—smaller clusters are put together while larger ones are divided up. Other descendants of Sangoaru are professionals working in many sectors and making significant contributions to the economy and welfare of the Maldives.

The names of these African slaves are interesting as well, especially since Sangoaru does not seem to have an Arabic etyma. Slaves usually took on Arabic names on conversion. No information about their African names or tribal origins is available. This is a problem, particularly for Indian Ocean migrants, due to the number of centuries that have elapsed since they came to Asia, and the slave dealers' lack of interest in such details. François Pyrard, a Frenchman, who was shipwrecked and spent several years in the Maldives during the seventeenth century, noticed that all the islanders had a single name; they did not have a surname or family name. In order to make a social distinction through names, the Maldivians use prefixes such as *Tacourou, Bybis, Callogues,* and *Camullogues.* The common folk have *Callo* and their craft or condition added alongside their personal name. Their wives and daughters are called Camulo (Gray 1887:217-218). It is noteworthy that the other four slaves had Arabic names.

In Sri Lanka, African migrants who came during the Portuguese era (1505–1658) from Mozambique or Goa appear to have learned the Indo-Portuguese of Ceylon. Contact languages usually evolve due to the sheer necessity for communication—and they are often learned relatively quickly. Since Indo-Portuguese was the mode of verbal communication between the Dutch and the Sri Lankans, the Afro-Sri Lankans had a linguistic advantage. Significantly, Indo-Portuguese became their mother-tongue, serving not only as the link language between the Africans and Europeans, but also between Africans of various ethnic origins who spoke to each other when grouped together by their colonial masters. Joseph Fernando, an African who was brought by a Frenchman from Mauritius and fought for the Kandyan king, spoke Indo-Portuguese of Ceylon during his interview. Indo-Portuguese continued to be a language of importance until about the mid-nineteenth century when English replaced it.

Farther East in Indonesia, Dutch and Malay were the lan-

Somali from Ayyal Ahmed Tribe
(Source: Renzo Manzoni,
El Yemeni tre anni nell'Arabie Felice.
Roma, 1884)

guages used in the Dutch colonial army. According to Van Kessel (2007:268), children of Ghanaian soldiers who grew up in barracks were mother-tongue speakers of Dutch, which would have helped them present a European or Dutch identity. However, when Indonesia regained independence, this only alienated the Afro-Indonesians from the Indonesians.

In Macau, Africans acted as interpreters between Europeans and Chinese, having lived there since the Portuguese presence (Mundy 1907). The recent African migrants to Hong Kong speak African languages—Twi, Igbo, Dagbami, Ewe, Ga, Kiswahili, Hausa, Kikuyu, Kinande, Lingala, and Zulu (Bodomo 2006). Settler-migrants tend to learn the local language, which enhances the processes of assimilation and indigenization.

CHAPTER 7

Reflections on African Displacement

The involuntary movement of Africans is a part of world history and economics. Given that migration is centuries old and historical accounts are sparse, it remains unknown how much of a problem language posed in the process of assimilation. Like other migrants, Africans may have communicated, to a large extent, through non-verbal means. The first generations of migrants who spoke an African language may have learned a lingua franca—Arabic, Swahili, Indo-Portuguese, or English. After a few preceding generations lived in Asia and became "indigenized," they would have learned the local language. Some Africans learned a western lingua franca as well as an Asian language—and they acted as interpreters between the indigenous people and European colonizers. For postcolonial nations that concentrated on strengthening national languages, there was little use for western languages at the grassroots level. However, the bourgeoisie, the new elite, and those who travel internationally on business spoke western languages. Contemporary economic pressures on new national regimes—that is, bringing in monetary returns and obtaining the basic necessities of life—influence what language Afro-Asians learn today. Once their generations are born locally, Africans begin to speak Asian languages. Today, Afro-Asians speak one or more of the following languages: Arabic, English, Gujarati, Hindi, Kannada, Konkani, Marathi, Sinhala, Sri Lanka Portuguese Creole (Indo-Portuguese of Ceylon), Tamil, Telugu, and Urdu.

As two of the most important cultural traits, religion and language are sometimes intertwined. For example, those who converted to Islam would have spoken Arabic, and Catholic converts spoke Portuguese, albeit in a creolized form. It appears that these two processes occurred at an early period of contact. Converts to Islam were freed and their progeny gradually assimilated into the host society. Learning colloquial Arabic would have been part of the acculturation process for Africans in the Middle East. In addition, Swahili could have served as a lingua franca between multilingual groups in Africa and between Europeans, Africans, and Asians. The diverse ethnic origins of the Afro-Asians, both from the interior and coast of Africa, meant that they needed a second language to communicate among themselves. This language could have been one that their owners or masters spoke or one that they had to learn in order to communicate.

Music and dance have generally been considered less important than language and religion. We should note, however, that the talents of Africans as musicians were recognized many centuries ago. More importantly, Africans have preserved their musical traditions within spirit possession ceremonies that they continued in their new homes. African music and instruments have become intertwined with the possession rituals, which are now not only practiced by Afro-Asians. Bava Gor, an Afro-Indian saint, has had an unusual impact on the Afro-Gujarati community in western India and elsewhere. His followers include Christian, Hindu, and Zoroasthrian Indians as well as his own kith and kin.

While the loss of African tribal names makes it impossible to trace the exact roots of the migrants, Afro-Asians can now be located globally, even after so many generations have lived in Asia, through DNA fingerprinting or their inherent musical abilities. Despite the many generations born in Asia, Afro-Asians have not changed their sense of rhythm and characteristic body movements. As subalterns with low socioeconomic status, they generally had no access to professional training. The choreography was not learned in a studio or ballroom, but in a garden. These art forms were usually learned by imitating adults during childhood, watching elders, and simply joining in. Since everyone participates in the sing-song sessions, it has become a communal activity that contributes to a collective identity.

Within Afro-Asian music and dance, memories of lost homes and habitats remain, even though the participating younger generation has no direct knowledge of that history. Passed along through oral tradition, their songs are repositories of poetic imagery—and a "database" for the languages spoken en route to their final destinations in Asia and during their period of service to European colonizers. Music and dance have generally been given less importance than language and religion by academics. However, the importance of music to migrants has gained recognition. The Africans of the Atlantic world have made their presence felt internationally through hybrid forms of music such as reggae, calypso, samba, blues, and jazz. In December 2004, I was fortunate to be in an audience of 1,400 at UNESCO Paris when Gilberto Gil, the Brazilian minister of culture, peformed hybrid songs that had evolved as a result of the transatlantic slave trade. This is a reminder: we must not forget the cultural contributions of Africans who unexpectedly became cultural brokers between continents.

Afro-Americans have broken the silence on African migration—and the benefits of this achievement are spreading to other regions of the world. The mapping of slave routes is important because it is part of the history of the slave trade and slavery. A case can be made for comparative studies on the Atlantic and Indian Oceans. We should not assume that the two oceans were mutually exclusive and that West Africans were transported to the Americas and East Africans were taken to Asia. There were exceptions to the general pattern. The Ghanaian soldiers who served in the Dutch colonial army in Indonesia, the Africans who were moved from Brazil to Goa, and the Mozambicans who were taken to Brazil are all examples. The Indian Ocean is not a closed system and there were movements from the Atlantic. Given that it is now impossible to break the wall of silence using case studies, by taking a multidisciplinary approach, we might, at least hope to piece together parts of this vast multi-dimensional puzzle.

The field of athletics is another area which could enhance the assimilation and integration of Afro-Asians. An experiment was carried out in Gujarat (India) but it was unsuccessful. Promising athletes were recruited by Indian companies to participate in inter-company sports meetings, but this reduced the number of Afro-Gujaratis in the sports camp. If economic incentives and adequate training are provided, Africans might represent Asian countries, not only at the national level but also internationally at the Olympics. In Europe and the Americas, they have excelled in these areas—and there is no reason why they cannot repeat the same performances in Asia.

In order to recognize the African presence in Asia, we must first reassess their contributions in a discussion about social and political issues. Making a comparison with transatlantic slavery is a good strategy since an emphasis has been placed on the wrong-doings and unethical deeds of its participants. The question of reparation is complicated because of internal and external participation in the slave trade. Nevertheless, imperial powers have to reassess their obligations and the legacy of their empires. They must find ways of assuaging the brutalities of the past. Colonization has ended, but obligations have not ceased. Although the Europeans who displaced Africans from their homelands no longer have a dominant presence in Asia, they could indicate ways in which Afro-Asians can now make contributions, not only nationally but internationally. They have an ethical obligation to do so. As mentioned earlier, sport is an area where Afro-Asians may excel as well as in music and dance. Even though these attempts may be several hundred years too late, they can still have some real effect on the quality of life for marginalized peoples.

How does the history of African migration to Asia differ from that to the Americas? Scholars need to address this question in the coming years. The multifaceted tasks that slaves performed in the East show that their histories in the East were also varied. In the Americas, slaves were generally restricted to plantations and mines. In the East, some slaves came into close contact with their masters or mistresses due to the nature of their work as domestic servants, seamstresses, nannies, concubines, and stewards. Others worked on the decks of ships as dock workers or divers in pearl fisheries.

Having African slaves in India was a matter of prestige; Indians never needed Africans as extra pairs of hands. Africans were a "luxury item" in a land where the supply of manpower was never a problem. Local people

The Ruins of the *Mahal* (Palace) in Janjira Fort
(Source: Kenneth X. Robbins & John McLeod, *African Elites in India:*
Habshi Amarat. Hyderabad: Mapin Publishing, 2006)

supplied Indian agricultural labor. There was no demand for Africans to
work as agricultural workers. However, the demand for good soldiers in
India, for defense purposes, was a major concern of Indian rulers who
were continuously threatened from neighboring rulers; in this area,
Africans had talents and reached great heights. The African dynasties of
Sachin and Janjira reveal their abilities. In some parts of Asia, African
slaves worked on agricultural farms as field foremen or overseers of shops.
Others worked as sailors on both military and merchant ships.

Due to the importance placed on military slaves in Islamic states,
some Africans were able to rise to the top of the hierarchy in India's
Muslim states, allowing them the opportunity to build their own military
empires. This also dismantled the social barriers between the African
military slave-soldier and the reigning Mughal emperors and their sul-
tanates. In addition, it paved the way for some Africans to form social
links and consolidate prestige and power. During most of the eighteenth

century and part of the nineteenth century, Afro-Indians in Janjira controlled India's west coast. The Dutch and the British had to negotiate alliances with the Afro-Asians in the nineteenth century. The African dynasties of Sachin and Janjira lasted until the mid-twentieth century; together with all the other princely states, they were abolished by the central government of India after independence from the British.

European slavery involved placing Africans into ideological systems that were unfamiliar. Many of them were converted to Christianity. Once the colonial powers withdrew from the East, these Africans were simply left behind in Asian cities, as can be seen in small pockets in India and Sri Lanka. Although the experience of conversion for the initial generation must have been traumatic, the descendants of Christian Afro-Asians benefited, at least in some places, due to their western cultural attributes. Unfortunately, their good fortune ended in decolonized nations where everything western began to be perceived as negative and a threat to national identity. The Europeans withdrew after Asian countries regained their independence, and the Africans were left without powerful protectors.

African migrants in Asia and their descendants have helped to dispel some of the assumptions that are made about slaves. Although the slave trade was an impetus for forced migration, all Africans in Asia are not without kinship or land. Moreover, they have maintained African cultural expressions, especially in music and dance. Although they have rarely retained African religious beliefs, they have maintained spirit possession practices. This appears to have resulted from active conversion to Christianity and Islam. Eastbound Africans were driven by two different forces: A more localized movement existed prior to western expansion in the Indian Ocean, and European activities in the Indian Ocean generally displaced Africans to lands beyond India and even as far as China.

Due to the huge gap in time it has taken to recognize an African presence in the East, it is now impossible to understand the degree of trauma that the migrants suffered, not only by being forcefully transported to places that were not of their choice, but also by having to abandon their beliefs. It was a one-way journey for eastward-bound Africans. As forced migrants and people with no control over their lives, they were unable

to return to Africa or keep their languages for very long because the eth-
nicities of the Africans were generally mixed.

The descendants of uprooted Africans and the history behind their
scattered presence in Asia should be incorporated into African diaspora
studies. The Indian Ocean is of much greater antiquity than the Atlantic.
In order to gain a comprehensive understanding of slavery and the slave
trade, systematic research on the various Afro-Asian communities in the
region must be undertaken. There is no single overarching model for
African displacement to Asia. Each Afro-Asian community has its own
history and therefore a different model is needed for each case.

References

Abbas, Z. 2002. *Pakistan's Sidi Keep Heritage Alive*. http://news.bbc.co.uk/2/hi/south_asia/1869876.stm

Al-Sābi, M. 1958. *Al-wuzara*. Cairo: Isa al-Babi al-Halabi.

Ali, A. A. 1966. *The Mughal Nobility under Aurangzeb*. Aligarh: Muslim University Press.

Alpers, E. 1997. The African Diaspora in the Northwestern Indian Ocean: Reconsideration of an Old Problem, New Directions for Research. *Comparative Studies of South Asia, Africa and the Middle East* 17 (2): 62–81.

———. 2003. Sailing into the Past: The African Experience in India. *Samar* 13.

———. 2003. The African Diaspora in the Indian Ocean: A Comparative Perspective. In *The African Diaspora in the Indian Ocean*, ed. S. de Silva Jayasuriya and R. Pankhurst. Trenton, NJ: Africa World Press.

———. 2004a. Escape from Slavery among Bonded Africans. In *The Structure of Slavery in Indian Ocean Africa and Asia*, ed. G. Campbell. London: Frank Cass.

———. 2004b. Flight to Freedom: Escape from Slavery among Bonded Africans in the Indian Ocean World, ca. 1750–1962. In *The Structure of Slavery in Indian Ocean Africa and Asia*, ed. G. Campbell. London: Frank Cass.

Aminaka, A. 2006. La place des Noires dans les Nanban Byoubu: Le potential des nanban Byouby comme documentation historique visuelle au Japan. *Cahiers des Anneaux de la Mémoire* 9: 221–230.

Anti-Slavery Reports. 1878. 21 (2), May 14.

Aubin, J. 1956. *Deux Sayyids de Bam au Xve siècle: contribution à l'histoire l'Iran timouride*. Wiesbaden: Franz Steiner Verlag GMBH.

Austin, R. 1989. The Nineteenth Century Islamic Slave Trade from East Africa (Swahili and Red Sea Coasts): A Tentative Census. In *Economics of the Indian Ocean Slave Trade*, ed. W. Clarence-Smith. London: Frank Cass.

Baca, S. 2004. UNESCO Newsletter. Paris: UNESCO.

Bacharach, J. L. 1981. African Military Slaves in the Medieval Middle East: The Cases of Iraq (869–955) and Egypt (868–1171). *International Journal of Middle Eastern Studies* 13: 471–495.

Badalkhan, S. 2006. On the Presence of African Musical Culture in Coastal Balochistan. In *Journeys and Dwellings: Indian Ocean Themes in South Asia*, ed. H. Basu. New Delhi: Orient Longman.

Banaji, D. R. 1932. *Bombay and the Siddis*. Bombay: Government Central Press.

Baptiste, F-A. 2006. Habshis au début du XIXe siècle L'Afghanistan: une note de recherché. *Cahiers des Anneaux de la Mémoire* 9: 109–120.

Baptiste, F-A., K. Robbins, and J. McLeod. 2006. Africans in the Medieval Deccan. In *African Elites in India*, ed. K. Robbins and J. McLeod. Hyderabad: Mapin Publishers.

Barendse, R. J. 1998. Slaving on the Malagasy Coast, 1640–1700. In *Cultures of Madagascar: Ebb and Flow Influences*. Leiden: IIAS Working Paper Series.

Basu, H. 1993. The Siddi and the Cult of Bava Gor in Gujarat. *Journal of Indian Anthropological Society* 28: 289–300.

———. 2003. Slave, Soldier, Trader, Faqir. In *The African Diaspora in the Indian Ocean*, ed. S. de Silva Jayasuriya and R. Pankhurst. Trenton, NJ: Africa World Press.

Bauss, R. 1997. The Portuguese Slave Trade from Mozambique to Portuguese India and Macau and Comments on Timor, 1750–1850: New Evidence from the Archives. *Camões Center Quarterly* 6/7: 1–2.

Beachey, R. W. 1976. *The Slave Trade of Eastern Africa*. London: Rex Collins.

Beckerleg, S. 2007. African Bedouin in Palestine. *African and Asian Studies* 6: 289–303.

Bengal Criminal Judicial Consultations. 1824. From Magistrates of Calcutta to W.B. Bayley, Chief Secretary to Government, dated 22

March. Bengal Criminal Judicial Consultations 28 of 25 March 1824.

Bennett, N. R. 1964. The CMS in Mombasa, 1873–1894. *Boston University Papers in African History*.

Bertolacci, A. 1817. *A View of the Agricultural, Commercial and Financial Interests of Ceylon*. London: Black, Parbury and Allen.

Bocarro, A. 1634. Livros das plantas de todas as fortalezas, cidades e povoações do Estado da Indian Oriental. In *Arquivo Português Oriental*, ed. A. B. de Bragança Pereira. Bastora, India Portuguesa: Rangel.

Bodomo, A. 2006. An Emerging African-Chinese Community in Hong Kong: The Case of Tsim Sha Tsui's Chungking Mansions. Paper submitted for the International Conference on The African Diaspora in Asia, Goa.

Bouketo, S. 2006. Les Habshis-Siddhis: une histoire en pointillés de la presence Africaine en Inde. *Cahiers des Anneaux de la Mémoire* 9: 151–170.

Boxer, C. R. 1968. *Fidalgos in the Far East, 1550–1770*. Oxford: Oxford University Press.

_____. 1969. *Four Centuries of Portuguese Expansion, 1415–1825: A Succinct Survey*. Johannesburg: Witwatersrand University Press.

Braudel, F. 1993. *A History of Civilizations*. Trans. R. Mayne. New York: Penguin Books.

British Sessional Papers. 1889. House of Commons: Correspondence Relating to the Slave Trade on the East African Coast 72 (88).

Brohier, P., trans. 1960. *A True and Exact Description of the Great Island of Ceylon by Revds Phillipus Baldaeus Published in Dutch in Amsterdam, 1672*. Dehiwala: Tisara Prakasakayo.

Brohier, R. L. 1973. *Discovering Ceylon*. Colombo: Lake House Investments.

Burkhardt, J. L. 1968. *Travels in Arabia*. 1829. Reprint, London: Routledge.

Burton, R. 1992. *Sindh and the Races that Inhabit the Valley of the Indus*. New Delhi: Asian Educational Services.

Burton-Page, J. 1971. Habshi. In *Encyclopedia of Islam*. London: Oxford University Press.

Camara, C. 2004. The Siddis of Uttara Kannada: History, Identity and

Change among African Descendants in Contemporary Karnataka. In *Sidis and Scholars*, ed. A. Catlin-Jairazbhoy and E. Alpers. New Delhi: Rainbow Publishers.

Camões, L. V. de. 1946–47. *Obras Completas*. Ed. Hernâni Cidade. Lisbon: Sá da Costa.

Campbell, G. 2004. Introduction: Slavery and Other Forms of Unfree Labour in the Indian Ocean World. In *The Structure of Slavery in Indian Ocean Africa and Asia*, ed. G. Campbell. London: Frank Cass.

Campbell, G., E. Alpers, and M. Salman, eds. 2007. Introduction. In *Resisting Bondage in the Indian Ocean World*. London and New York: Routledge.

Carreira, E. 1998. India. In *Nova Historia da Expansão Portuguesa, 10, O Império Africano 1825–1890*, ed. V. Alexandre and J. Dias. Lisbon: Editorial Estampa.

Catlin-Jairazbhoy, A. 2006. From Sufi Shrines to the World Stage: African Indian Music in Sidi Goma Tours 2002–2006. *MUSIKE* 3: 1–24.

Catlin-Jairazbhoy, A., and E. A. Alpers, eds. 2004. *Sidis and Scholars*. Delhi: Rainbow Publishers.

Chattopadhyay, A. R. 1963. Slavery in the Bengal Presidency Under East India Company Rule, 1772–1843. PhD diss., University of London.

Chauhan, R. R. S. 1995. *Africans in India: From Slavery to Royalty*. New Delhi: Asian Publication Services.

Christensen, D. 2002. Musical Life in Sohar, Oman. In *The Garland Encyclopedia of World Music: The Middle East*, ed. V. Danielson, S. Marcus and D. Reynolds. New York: Routledge.

Collins, R. 2006. The African Slave Trade to Asia and the Indian Ocean Islands. *African & Asian Studies* 3-4: 325–347.

Contenson, H. de. 1965. Les Fouilles à Haoulti en 1959. *Annales d'Ethiopie 5*.

Cook, E. 1953. *Ceylon: Its Geography, Its Resources and Its People*. London: MacMillan & Company Ltd.

Coupland, R. 1933. *The British Anti-Slavery Movement*. London: Oxford University Press.

Covarrubias, S. de. 1943. *Tesoro de la lengua castellana o española, según la impression de 1611, con las adiciones de Benito Remigio Noydens publicasas en la de 1674*. Ed. M. de Riquer. Barcelona: Horta.

Cummins, J. S. 1962. *The Travels and Controversies of Friar Domingo Navarrete, 1618–1686*. Cambridge: Cambridge University Press.

Cunna, L. 2007. Personal Communication.

Dalai, P. V. D. 1839. The Evidence of Pandit Vishnu Datta Dalai. Appendix 1, Law Commissioner's Reports and Evidence on Slavery in the East Indies.

Dalby, D. 1970. The Place of Africa and Afro-America in the History of the English Language. *African Language Review* 9: 280–297.

Darlington, C. D. 1979. *The Evolution of Man and Society*. London: George Allen & Unwin.

Dayal, J. 2007. Personal Communication.

De Barros, J. 1638. *Decadas da Asia*. Lisboa.

De Haan, F. 1922, 1935. VOC 4026: Rôle des servants du comptoir de Pondicherry. *Oud Batavia* 1: 145–172.

De Silva, C. R. 1953. *Ceylon under the British Occupation, 1795–1833*. Colombo: Apothecaries Company.

De Silva, C. R. 1972. *The Portuguese in Ceylon, 1617–1638*. Colombo: H. W. Cave & Company.

De Silva Jayasuriya, S. 1995. Portuguese and English Translations of Some Indo- Portuguese Songs in the Hugh Nevill Collection. *Journal of the Royal Asiatic Society Sri Lanka* XL: 1–102.

_____. 1996. Indo-Portuguese Songs of Sri Lanka. The Nevill Manuscript. *Bulletin of the School of Oriental & African Studies* 59 (2): 253–267.

_____. 1997a. Hugh Nevill Collection of Indo-Portuguese Verses: Portuguese and English Translations of Oersaan and Falentine. *Journal of the Royal Asiatic Society Sri Lanka* XLII: 107–211.

_____. 1997b. A Nineteenth-Century Portuguese Creole Text. University of London Seminar Series on Pidgins and Creoles, School of Oriental & African Studies, 4 December.

_____. 1999–2001. Hugo Schuchardt Manuscript of Sri Lanka Portuguese Creole: Linguistic Analysis with Portuguese and English

Translations. *ORBIS* 41:183–197.

_____. 1999a. On the Indo-Portuguese of Ceylon: A Translation of a Hugo Schuchardt Manuscript. *Portuguese Studies* 15: 52–69.

_____. 1999b. Echoes of the Tagus: Music of Sri Lanka. *Indian Ocean Review* 12 (1): 18.

_____. 1999c. Portuguese in Sri Lanka: Effects of Substratum Languages. *Journal of the Royal Asiatic Society of Great Britain and Ireland* 9 (2): 251–270.

_____. 1999d. Sinhala Borrowings in Sri Lanka Portuguese Creole. *Journal of the Royal Asiatic Society of Sri Lanka* 44: 31–37.

_____. 1999e. Reduplication in Asian Portuguese Creoles. Creolistics Workshop, University of Westminster, London, 9–11 April.

_____. 1999f. Tense Mood Aspect Markers in Asian Portuguese Creoles: A Comparison. Paper presented at the Third Association of Linguistics Typology Conference University of Amsterdam, The Netherlands, 26–28 August.

_____. 2000a. English Borrowings in Sri Lanka Portuguese Creole. ESSE 5 Conference, University of Helsinki, Finland, 28 August.

_____. 2000b. Portuguese Folk Literature in Sri Lanka. In *Luso-Asian Voices*, ed. D. Brookshaw and C. Willis. Bristol: University of Bristol Press.

_____. 2000c. Sri Lanka Portuguese Creole: A Language in Eclipse. *Indian Ocean Review* 13 (1): 20–21.

_____. 2000d. Indo-Portugués e Sinhala: Inter-Câmbio das Palavras. *PAPIA* 10: 66–77.

_____. 2000e. Sri Lanka Portuguese Creole Verses. *EPISTEME* 5-6: 313–315.

_____. 2000f. Sri Lankan Malay Creole: Unique Malay. Paper presented at the International Symposium on Malay/Indonesian Linguistics held in Jakarta, Indonesia, 26–27 July.

_____. 2000g. Portuguese Cultural Imprint on Sri Lanka. *LUSOTOPIE* 253–259.

_____. 2001a. Les Cafres de Ceylan: le chaînon portugais. *Cahiers des Anneax de la Mémoire* 3: 229–253.

_____. 2001b. *An Anthology of Indo-Portuguese Verse*. United Kingdom: Edwin Mellen Press.

_____. 2001c. *Tagus to Taprobane: Portuguese Impact on the Socioculture of Sri Lanka from 1505 AD*. The Ceylon Historical Journal Monograph Series, Vol. 20. Dehiwela: Tisara Publishers.

_____. 2001d. *Indo-Portuguese of Ceylon: A Contact Language*. London: Athena Publications.

_____. 2001e. Asian Portuguese Creoles: A Common Origin. *EPISTEME* 7-8-9: 459–466.

_____. 2001f. A Unique Malay: Sri Lankan Malay Creole. *NUSA* 50:43–52.

_____. 2002a. The Ceylon *Kaffirs*: A Creole Community in an Indian Ocean Island. Paper presented at the Conference on Cultural Exchange and Transformation in the Indian Ocean World, USA, University of California Los Angeles, 5–6 April.

_____. 2002b. The Portuguese Encounter with Sri Lanka: A Musical Interface. *EPISTEME* 10-11-12: 173–189.

_____. 2002c. Reduplication in Indo-Portuguese, Malayo-Portuguese and Sino-Portuguese. In *Twice as Meaningful*, ed. S. Kouwenberg. London: Battlebridge Publications.

_____. 2002d. Grammatical Variation in an Indo-Portuguese Creole. *ORBIS* 42.

_____. 2003a. The African Diaspora in Sri Lanka. In *The African Diaspora in the Indian Ocean*, ed. S. de Silva Jayasuriya and R. Pankhurst. Trenton, NJ: Africa World Press.

_____. 2003b. Les femmes et l'esclavage au Sri Lanka. *Cahiers des Anneaux de la Mémoire* 5: 99–122.

_____. 2003c. The Portuguese Encounter with Sri Lanka. Paper presented at the Conference on Culture, Colonisation and Decolonisation: French, Portuguese, Spanish and Dutch Perspectives, Institute of Romance Studies, Institute of Historical Research and Institute of Latin American Studies, University of London. 21–22 February.

_____. 2003d. Jorge de Sena's Cantiga de Ceilão: Brazilian Reflections. Paper presented at the Institute of Latin American Studies, University of London. 1 November.

_____. 2003e. Cantiga de Ceilão and Jorge de Sena: Portuguese Reflections. Paper presented at King's College London, University of London. 12 November.

_____. 2003f. Changing Political Scenarios and Linguistic Innovation: The Case of Sri Lanka Portuguese Creole. *Sprachtypol. Univ. Forsch. (STUF)* 56 (4): 400–411.

_____. 2003g. Malay Contacts with Sri Lanka. International Institute for Asian Studies Newsletter, University of Leiden.

_____. 2004a. Trading on a Thalassic Network. Paper presented at the International Conference on Issues of Memory: Coming to Terms with the Slave Trade and Slavery, UNESCO, Paris, 3–5 December.

_____. 2004b. La Musique Créole Portugaise du Sri Lanka. In *Métissages Culturels et Créativité*, ed. R. de Villanova and G. Vermès. Paris: L'Harmattan.

_____. 2004c. Baila: A Cross Cultural Composition. Paper presented at the British Forum of Ethnomusicology Annual Conference at the Elphinstone Institute, University of Aberdeen, Scotland, 15–18 April.

_____. 2004d. Portuguese Musical Legacies in the World: *Baila, Kaffrinha, Joget, Kroncong*. Paper presented at King's College London, University of London, 27 November.

_____. 2004e. Tense Mood and Aspect in Sri Lanka Portuguese Creole. *Journal of the Royal Asiatic Society, Sri Lanka* XLVII: 115–132.

_____. 2005a. The Portuguese Identity of the Afro-Sri Lankans. *LUSO-TOPIE* 12 (1/2).

_____. 2005b. Indian Ocean Island Cultures: African Migration and Identity. *Zanzibar International Film Festival Journal* 2:22–29.

_____. 2005c. Jorge de Sena on Portuguese Ballads. *EPISTEME* 13–14.

_____. 2005d. Sri Lankan Romanceiros and the Goan Mando. Paper presented at the Conference on Music and the Art of Seduction, Organized by the Dutch Society for Ethnomusicology and World Music and the Amsterdam School of Cultural Analysis, University of Amsterdam, 19–22 May.

_____. 2005e. Music and Dance in Identity Formation. Paper presented at the British Forum of Ethnomusicology Annual Conference at the School of Oriental and African Studies, and AHRB Centre for Cross-Cultural Dance and Music Research, University of London, 12–15 April.

_____. 2005f. Linguistic Flows and Identity. Paper presented at the Conference on Portugal and Sri Lanka: 500 Years organized and held at the Calouste Gulbenkian Cultural Centres of Paris, 15–17 December.

_____. 2006a. Identifying Africans in Asia: What's in a Name? *African & Asian Studies* 6: 275–303 .

_____. 2006b. Trading on a Thalassic Network: African Migrations across the Indian Ocean. *International Social Sciences Journal* 188: 215–226.

_____. 2006c. Les Afro-Sri Lankais: Liens et Racines. *Cahiers des Anneaux de la Mémoire* 9: 171–188.

_____. 2006d. Music and Memories: Oral Traditions from an Indian Ocean Island. *MUSIKE* 3:25–42.

_____. 2006e. Malay Navigators and Culture Crossings in the Indian Ocean. Paper presented at the Conference on "Indian Ocean: Cultures in Contact" held at the Institute of Commonwealth Studies, University of London, July 14.

_____. 2007a. A Forgotten Minority: The Afro-Sri Lankans. *African and Asian Studies* 6: 227–242.

_____. 2007b. Portugal and Sri Lanka: Sociocultural Interactions and Language Contact. *Oriente* 17: 3–18.

_____. 2007c. Migrants and the Maldives. Paper presented at the Conference on Migrants and the Making of Indian Ocean Cultures. School of Oriental & African Studies, July 11.

_____. 2008. *Portuguese in the East: Cultural History of a Maritime Trading Empire*. London: I. B. Tauris Academic Publishers.

De Silva Jayasuriya, S., and R. Wijetunge. 1998. Portuguese Borrowings in Sinhala. *Journal of the Royal Asiatic Society, Sri Lanka* XLIII: 1–12.

De Silva Jayasuriya, S., and R. Pankhurst. 2003. On the African Diaspora in the Indian Ocean. In *The African Diaspora in the Indian Ocean*, ed. S. de Silva Jayasuriya and R. Pankhurst. Trenton, NJ: Africa World Press.

De Souza, T. 1989. French Slave-Trading in Portuguese Goa (1773–1791). In *Essays in Goan History*, ed. T. de Souza. New Delhi: Concept Publishing House.

_____. 2004. Slave Trade in Goa. *Parmal* 3: 43–49.

Dos Martines Lopes, M. de J. 1996. *Goa Setecentista: Tradição e Moderni-dade (1750–1800)*. Lisboa: Universidade Católica Portuguesa.

Drewal, H. 2004. Aliens and Homelands: Identity, Agency and the Arts among the Siddis of Uttara Kannada. In *Siddis and Scholars*. Delhi: Rainbow Publishers.

Durugonul, E. 2003. The Invisibility of Turks of African Origin and the Construction of Turkish Cultural Identity: The Need for a New Historiography. *Journal of Black Studies* 33: 281–294.

Eaton, R. 2006. Malik Ambar and Elite Slavery in the Deccan, 1440–1650. In *African Elites in India*, ed. K. Robbins and J. McLeod. Hyderabad: Mapin Publishers.

Edwardes, S. M. 1910. *The Gazeteer of Bombay City and Island*. Bombay: Times Press.

Eltis, D. 1979. The British Contribution to the Nineteenth Century Transatlantic Slave Trade. *Economic History Review* 32(2): 211.

_____. 1986. Fluctuations in the Age and Sex Ratios of Slaves in the Nineteenth-Century Transatlantic Slave Traffic. *Slavery and Abolition* 7: 257–272.

Eriksen, T. H. 1999. Tu dimunn pu vini kreol: The Mauritian creole and the concept of creolization. Lecture presented at the University of Oxford.

Ewald, J. 2000. Crossers of the Sea: Slaves, Freedmen, and Other Migrants in the Northwestern Indian Ocean, ca. 1750–1914. *American Historical Review* 105: 69-91.

Fentress, J., and C. Wickham. 1992. *Social Memory*. Oxford: Blackwell.

Fernando, C. M. 1894. The Music of Ceylon. *Journal of the Royal Asiatic Society* (Ceylon) 13: 83–189.

Forbes, A., and F. Ali. 1980. The Maldive Islands and their Historical Links with the Coast of Eastern Africa. *Kenya Past and Present* 2.

Foster, W. ed. 1968. *Early Travels in India, 1593–1619*. New Delhi: S. Chand & Company.

Freeman-Grenville, G. S. P. 1971. The Sidi and Swahili. *Bulletin of the British Association of Orientalists*, n.s., 6: 3–18.

Gerbeau, H. 1979. The Slave Trade in the Indian Ocean: Problems Facing the Historian and Research to be Undertaken. In *The African*

Slave Trade from the Fifteenth to the Nineteenth Century. Paris: UNESCO.

_____. 1986. Engagees and Coolies on Réunion Island: Slavery's Masks and Freedom's Constraints. In *Colonialism and Migration: Indentured Labour Before and After Slavery,* ed. P. C. Emmer. Dordrecht, Boston and Lancaster: Martinus Nijhoff Publishers.

Germain, A. 1868. Quelques mots sur l'Oman et le sultan de Maskate. *Bulletin de la Société de Géographie* (Paris), 5e série, 6.

Gibb, H. A. R. 1929. *Ibn Batuta, Travels in Asia and Africa and Asia, 1325–1354.* London: Routledge.

Githige, R. H. 1986. The Issue of Slavery. *Journal of Religion in Africa* XVI (3): 209–225.

Gray, A. 1887. *The Voyage of François Pyrard of Laval to the East Indies, the Maldives, the Moluccas and Brazil.* London: Hakluyt Society.

Hagerdähl, H. 2007. Personal Communication.

Hall, S. 1996. Who Needs Identity? In *Questions of Cultural Identity,* ed. S. Hall and P. du Gay. London: Sage Publications.

Hamers, J. F., and M. H. A. Blanc. 1983. *Bilinguality and Bilingualism.* Cambridge: Cambridge University Press.

Hampton, B., and C. Sykes. 1995. African American Secular and Sacred Music. *The JVC Smithsonian/Folkways Video Anthology of Music and Dance of the Americas,* ed. M. Greenberg. Washington D.C.: JVC Smithsonian Folkways Records.

Hardy, S. 1864. *Jubilee Memorials of the Wesleyan Mission, South Ceylon, 1814–1864.* Colombo: Wesleyan Mission Press.

Harris, J. 1971. *The African Presence in Asia: Consequences of the East African Slave Trade.* Evanston, IL: Northwestern University Press.

_____. 2003. Expanding the Scope of African Diaspora Studies: The Middle East and India. *Radical History Review* 87: 157–168.

Hassan, S. Q. 2002. Musical Instruments in the Arab World. In *The Garland Encyclopedia of World Music: The Middle East,* ed. V. Danielson, S. Marcus, and D. Reynolds. New York: Routledge.

Holm, J. 1989. *Pidgins and Creoles.* Cambridge: Cambridge University Press.

Houbert, J. 2003. Creolisation and Decolonisation in the Changing

Geopolitics of the Indian Ocean, ed. S. de Silva Jayasuriya and R. Pankhurst. *The African Diaspora in the Indian Ocean.* Trenton, NJ: Africa World Press.

Huntingford, G. B. 1980., trans. and ed. *The Periplus of the Red Sea.* London: Hakluyt Society.

Hunwick, J. 1978. Black Africans in the Islamic World: An Understudied Dimension of the Black Diaspora, *Tarikh* 5 (4).

_____. 2004. The Religious Practices of Black Slaves in the Mediterranean Islamic World. In *Slavery on the Frontiers of Islam,* ed. P. Lovejoy. Princeton: Markus Wiener.

Inalcik, H., and D. Quartaert, eds. 1994. *An Economic and Social History of the Ottoman Empire, 1300–1914.* New York and Cambridge: Cambridge University Press.

Ingrams, H. 1942. *Arabia and the Isles.* London: John Murray.

Ingrams, L. 2006. African Connections in Yemeni Music. *MUSIKE* 3: 65–76.

Jasdanwalla, F. 2007. Personal Communication.

Johnson, Y. 1939. *A Standard Swahili-English Dictionary.* London: Oxford University Press.

Jolly, J. 1876. *Naradiya Dharmasastra of the Institutes of Narada.* London: Trubner & Company.

Jones, J. W., trans. 1863. *Travels of Ludovico di Varthema in Egypt, Syria, Arabia Deserta and Arabia Felix, in Persia, India and Ethiopia, AD 1503 to 1508.* Ed. G. P. Badger. London: Hakluyt Society.

Kasruri, E. 2002. The Black Dutchmen: African Soldiers in the Netherlands East Indies. In *Merchants, Missionaries and Migrants: 300 Years of Dutch-Ghanaian Relations,* ed. I. Van Kessel. Accra: Sub-Saharan Publishers.

Kassebaum, G., and P. Clause. 2000. Karnataka. In *The Garland Encyclopedia of World Music,* ed. Alison Arnold. New York: Routledge.

Kemp, A., and R. Reichmann. 2003. Foreign Workers in Israel. Working Paper 13, Adva Center [Hebrew], Tel Aviv.

Khalidi, O. 1988. African Diaspora in India: The Case of the Habashis of the Dakan. *Hambard Islamicus* XI (4): 3–22.

_____. 2006. The Habshis of Hyderabad. In *African Elites in India,* ed. K.

X. Robbins and J. McLeod. Hyderabad: Mapin Publishers.

Khalifa, A. 2006a. African Influences on Culture and Music in Dubai. *International Social Sciences Journal* 188,:227–236.

———. 2006b. Spirit Possession and its Practices in Dubai, United Arab Emirates. *MUSIKE* 3: 43–64.

Knox, R. 1681. *An Historical Relation of the Island Ceylon*. Dehiwela: Tisara Prakasakayo Ltd.

Kusruri, E. 2002. Reminiscences of the African community in Purworejo, Indonesia. In *Merchants, Missionaries & Migrants*, ed. I. Van Kessel. Accra: Sub-Saharan Publishers.

La Rue, G. M. 2004. The Frontiers of Enslavement: Bagirmi and the Trans-Saharan Slave Routes. In *Slavery on the Frontiers of Islam*, ed. P. Lovejoy. Princeton, NJ: Markus Wiener Publishers.

Lévi-Strauss, C. 1972. *Structural Anthropology*. Trans. Claire Jackbson and Brooke Grundfest Schoepf. Hammondsworth: Penguin.

Levtzion, N. 1977. The Western Maghrib and Sudan. In *The Cambridge History of Africa*, ed. Roland Oliver. Cambridge: Cambridge University Press.

Lewis, B. 1971. *Race and Color in Islam*. New York: Harper Torchbooks, Harper Row Publishers.

Linschoten, J. 1885. The *Voyage of John Huyghen Van Linschoten to the East Indies*. Ed. A. C. Burnell and P. A. Tiele. London: Hakluyt Society.

Lodhi, A. Y. 2000. *Oriental Influences in Swahili: A Study in Languages and Culture Contacts*. Göteborg: Acta Universitatis Gothoburgensis.

Lombard, M. 1971. *L'Islam dans sa première grandeur (VIIIe–XIe siècle)*. Paris: Flammarion.

Lovejoy, P. 1983. *Transformations in Slavery: A History of Slavery in Africa*. Cambridge: Cambridge University Press.

———. 2004a. Slavery, the Bilād al-Sūdān and the Frontiers of the African Diaspora. In *Slavery on the Frontiers of Islam*, ed. P. Lovejoy. Princeton, NJ: Markus Wiener Publishers.

———. 2004b. Muslim Freedmen in the Atlantic World: Images of Manumission and Self-Redemption. In *Slavery on the Frontiers of Islam*, ed. P. Lovejoy. Princeton, NJ: Markus Wiener Publishers.

Machado, P. 2004. A Forgotten Corner of the Indian-Ocean: Gujarati Merchants, Portuguese India and the Mozambique Slave-Trade, c. 1730–1830. In *The Structure of Slavery in Indian Ocean Africa and Africa*, ed. G. Campbell. London: Frank Cass.

Maloney, C. 1980. *People of the Maldive Islands*. Madras: Orient Longman.

Marjumdar, R. C. 1960. *The History and Culture of the Indian People: The Delhi Sultanate*. Bombay: MacMillan.

Marmon, S. 1995. *Eunuchs and Sacred Boundaries in Islamic Society*. New York and Oxford: Oxford University Press.

Matthews, D., and A. Mordini. 1959. The Monastery of Debra Damo, Ethiopia. *Archaeologia* 97.

McCrindle, J. W., trans. 1897. *The Christian Topography of Cosmas, an Egyptian Monk*. London: Hakluyt Society.

Medeiros, E. 2003. Contribution of the Mozambican Diaspora in the Development of Cultural Identities in the Indian Ocean Islands. In *The African Diaspora in the Indian Ocean*, ed. S. de Silva Jayasuriya and R. Pankhurst. Trenton, NJ: Africa World Press.

Mendes Corea, A. A. 1994. *Timor Português: Contribuções para o seu astado antropologico*. Lisboa: Imprensa Nacional.

Micklem, J. 2001. *Sidis in Gujarat*. Edinburgh: Centre of African Studies, Edinburgh University.

Miers, S. 2004. Slavery: A Question of Definition. In *The Structure of Slavery in Indian Ocean Africa and Asia*, ed. G. Campbell. London: Frank Cass.

Minda, A. 2007. Dynamics of Ethnic Identity among the Siddis of Hyderabad. *African and Asian Studies* 6: 321–345.

Mirzai, B. 2005. The Slave Trade and the African Diaspora in Iran. *ZIFF Journal* 2: 30–34.

_____. 2006. Le commerce des esclaves africains dans l'Iran du XIXe siècle. *Cahiers des Anneaux de la Mémoire* 9: 29–42.

Moffett, E., ed. 1958. *Handbook Tanbanyika*. Dar-es-Salaam: Government Printer.

Mohamed, N. 2006. *Essays on Early Maldives*. Male: National Centre for Linguistic and Historical Research.

Moniz, A. F. 1923. *Noticias e Documentos para a Historia de Damão*. Bastora.

_____. 2000. *Noticias e Documentos para a Historia de Damão*. Lisboa: Associação Fraternidade Damão-Diu e Simpatizantes.

More, H. 1827. *The Feast of Freedom or the Abolition of Domestic Slavery in Ceylon*. London: T. Cadell.

Moutou, B. 1985. Tares et sêquelles de l'esclavage a l'Ile Maurice et a l'Ile Rodrigues. Paper presented at International Seminar on Slavery in the South-West Indian Ocean, Mahatma Gandhi Institute, Maka-Mauritius, 26 February to 2 March.

Mundy, P. 1907. *The Travels of Peter Mundy in Europe and Asia, 1608–1667*. Cambridge: Hakluyt Society.

Newitt, M. 2003. Madagascar and the African Diaspora. In *The African Diaspora in the Indian Ocean*, eds. S. de Silva Jayasuriya and R. Pankhurst. Trenton, NJ: Africa World Press.

Nicolini, B. 2006. The Makran-Baluch-African Network in Zanzibar and East Africa during the XIX century. *African and Asian Studies* 5 (3-4): 347–370.

Obeng, P. 2007a. Service to God, Service to Master/Client: African Indian Military Contribution to Karnataka. *African and Asian Studies* 6: 271–288.

_____. 2007b. Personal Communication.

Patel, J. 2004. The Sidis of Gujarat and the Quest for Human Dignity. In *Sidis and Scholars*, ed. A. Catlin-Jairazbhoy and E. Alpers. India: Rainbow Publishers.

Pearson, M. N. 1990. *Slavery in Coastal India*. Cambridge: Cambridge University Press.

Pélissier, R. 1996. *Timor en guerre: le crocodile et les Portugais, 1847–1913*. Orgeval: R. Pélissier.

Pereira, C. 2006. Les Africains de Bombay et la colonie de Freretown. *Cahiers des Anneaux de la Mémoire* 9: 231–250.

Pieris, P. E. 1909. *Ribeiro's History of Ceilão*. Colombo: Apothecaries & Company Ltd.

_____. 1973. Some Documents Relating to the Rise of the Dutch Power in Ceylon, 1602–1670, from the Translations at the India Office, London.

Pieters, S., ed and trans. 1911. *Memoir of Hendrik Zwaardecroon*. Colombo.

Pineo, H. K. 1979. Aperçu d'une immigration forcée: L'importation d'Africains libérés aux Mascareignes et aux Seychelles, 1840–1880. In *Minoritiés et gens de mere en ocean indien, XIXe–XXe siècles*, IHPOM Etudes et Documents 12. Université de Provence: Institut d'histoire des pays d'outre-mer.

Pinto, J. 2006. The African Native in Indiaspora. *African and Asian Studies* 5 (3-4): 383–397.

Pipes, D. 1981. *Slave Soldiers and Islam: The Genesis of a Military System*. New Haven and London: Yale University Press.

Pires, T. 1944. *The Suma Oriental of Thomé Pires: An Account of the East, from the Red Sea to Japan, Written in Malacca and India in 1512–1515*. London: Hakluyt Society.

Planhil, X. 1958. *De la plaine Pamphylienne aux lacs Pisidiens. Nomadisme et vie paysanne [Of the Pamphilian Plan and the Pisidian lakes]*. Paris: Librarie Adrien-Maisonneuve.

Popovic, A. 1976. *Le révolte des esclaves en Iraq au IIIe/IXe siècle*. Paris: Geuthner.

_____. 1999. *The Revolt of African Slaves in Iraq in the 3rd/9th Century*. Princeton, NJ: Markus Wiener Publishers.

Powell, G. 1973. *The Kandyan Wars: The British Army in Ceylon 1803–1818*. London: Lee Cooper.

Racy, A. J. 1992. The lyre of the Arab Gulf: Historical roots, Geographical Links, and the Local Context. *Al-Ma'thurat al-sha'biyyah* 27:7–17.

_____. 2002. Overview of Music in the Mashriq. In *The Garland Encyclopedia of World Music: The Middle East*, ed. V. Danielson, S. Marcus and D. Reynolds. New York: Routledge.

_____. 2006. In the Path of the Lyre: The Tanburah of the Gulf Region. *MUSIKE* 3:92–122.

Rae, K. B. 2004. *Nobi*: A Korean System of Slavery. In *The Structure of Slavery in Indian Ocean African and Asia*, ed. G. Campbell. London: Frank Cass.

_____. 2006. African Presence in Korea. Paper submitted for the International Conference on the African Diaspora in Asia, Goa.

Ranasinha, A. G. 1950. *Census of Ceylon 1946*. Colombo: Ceylon

Government Press.

Ravenshaw, J. G. 1801. Collector South Canara to George Garrow, Acting Secretary Board of Revenue, 12 August.

Resende, G. de 1516. Cancionera Geral, ed. A. J. Gonçalvez Guimarãis. Coimbra.

Ricks, T. M. 1988. Slaves and Slave Trading in Shi'I Iran, 1500–1900. Paper presented at the annual meeting of the American Historical Association, Cincinnati.

Ricks, T. 1989. Slaves and Slave Traders in the Persian Gulf, Eighteenth and Nineteenth Centuries: An Assessment. In *Economics of the Indian Ocean Slave Trade*, ed. W. Clarence-Smith. London: Frank Cass.

Robbins, K., and J. McLeod. 2006. *African Elites in India: Habshi Amarat.* Hyderabad: Mapin Publishers.

Roberts, M., I. Raheem, and P. Colin-Thome, 1989. *People Inbetween.* Ratmalana: Sarvodaya Book Publishing Services.

Sabar, G., and K. Shlomit. 2006. Between the Local and the Global: African Musicians in Israel. *Musike* 3: 77–96.

Sabben-Clare, E. E. 1945. African Troops in Asia. *African Affairs* 44: 151–157.

Sadiq Ali, S. 1996. *The African Dispersal in the Deccan.* Hyderabad: Orient Longman.

Sangustine, F. 1980. Un aide-mémoire à l'usage de l'acheteur d'esclaves. Thése doctorat, Université de Paris III.

Sarhar, J. 1955. *House of Shivaji: Studies and Documents on Maratha History.* Calcutta: M. C. Sarhar & Sons.

Sarkar, T. 1985. Bondage in the Colonial Context. In *Chains of Servitude: Bondage and Slavery in India.* ed. U. Patnaik and M. Dingwaney. Madras: Sangam Books.

Saunders, A. C. de C. M. 1982. *A Social History of Black Slaves and Freedmen in Portugal, 1441–1555.* Cambridge: Cambridge University Press.

Schurhammer, G. 1977. *Francis Xavier, His Life, His Times.* Rome: The Jesuit Historical Institute.

Segal, R. 2001. *Islam's Black Slaves: The Other Black Diaspora.* New York: Farrar, Straus & Giroux.

Serjeant, R. B. 1987. Some Observations on African Slaves in Arabia. Paper presented at the workshop on the long-distance trade in slaves across the Indian Ocean and the Red Sea in the nineteenth century. School of Oriental and African Studies, University of London, 17–19 December.

Shepherd, J., and P. Wicke. 1997. *Music and Cultural Theory*. UK: Polity Press.

Sheriff, A. 2005. The Twilight of Slavery in the Persian Gulf. *ZIFF Journal* 2:35–45.

Sherwood, M. 2007. *After Abolition*. London: I. B. Tauris Academic Publishers.

Shirodkar, P. P. 1985. Slavery in Coastal India. In *Purabhilekh-Puratatva, Journal of the Directorate of Archives, Archaeology and Museum* 3 (1):36–37.

Shroff, B. 2007. Sidis in Mumbai: Negotiating Identities between Mumbai and Gujarat. *African and Asian Studies* 6:305–319.

Stein, P. 1997. The English Language in Mauritius: Past and Present. In *English World-Wide* 18 (1):65–89.

Stone, R. 1998. African Music in a Constellation of Arts. In *The Garland Encyclopedia of Music*. ed. R. Stone. New York: Garland Publishing Inc.

Tadmor, U. 2005. Personal Communication.

Talib, Y., and F. Samir. 1989. The African Diaspora in Asia. In *UNESCO General History of Africa*, ed. M. El Fasi. Berkeley: University of California Press.

Tambs-Lyche, H. 1997. *Power, Profit and Poetry: Traditional Society in Kathiawar, Western India*. New Delhi: Manohar Publishers.

Teelock, V. C. 1999. The Influence of Slavery in the Formation of Creole Identity. *Comparative Studies of South Asia, Africa and the Middle East* XIX (2): 3–8.

The India Gazette and Calcutta Public Advertiser 307. 1786 (2 October). Repeated in 309 (16 October).

Thomas, H. 1997. *The Slave Trade*. London: Picador.

Thompson, T. L. 1998. Hidden Histories and the Problem of Ethnicity in Palestine. In *Western Scholarship and the History of Palestine*, ed. M.

Prior. London: Melisende.

Topp-Fargion, J. 1992. Women and the Africanization of Taarab in Zanzibar. PhD diss., University of London.

Trotman, D. V., and P. Lovejoy. 2004. Community of Believers: Trinidad Muslims and the Return to Africa, 1810–1850. In *Slavery on the Frontiers of Islam*. Princeton, NJ: Markus Wiener Publishers.

Van den Berg, L. W. C. 1886. *Le Hadhramaut et les Colonies Arbes dans l'archipel Indien*. Batavia.

Van der Biesen, I. 2006. Interpénétrations culturelles et transition d'un système économique La diaspora de l'Afrique de l'Est et le Gujarat dans une perspective historico-anthropologique. *Cahiers des Anneaux de la Mémoire* 9:121–150.

Van Kessel, I. 2002. The Black Dutchmen: African Soldiers in the Netherlands East Indies. In *Merchants, Missionaries and Migrants: 300 Years of Dutch-Ghanaian Relations*, ed. I. Van Kessel. Accra: Sub-Saharan Publishers.

_____. 2006. Aux Indes néerlandaises: des Africains, agents de police, militaries, exiles et un prince. *Cahiers des Anneaux de la Mémoire* 9: 189–220.

_____. 2007. Belanda Hitam: the Indo-African Communities in Java. *African and Asian Studies* 6: 243–279.

Vernet, T. 2006. Les réseaux de traite de l'Afrique orientale: côte Swahili, Comores et Nord-Ouest de Madagascar (vers 1500–1750). *Cahiers des Anneaux de la Mémoire* 9: 67–108.

Vijayakumar, M., and K.C. Malhotra.1983. Inbreeding and Matrimonial Distances among the Siddis of Karnataka. *Current Anthropology* 24 (2): 228–9.

Vink, M. 2003. "The World's Oldest Trade": Dutch Slavery and Slave Trade in the Indian Ocean in the Seventeenth Century. *Journal of World History* 14 (2): 131–177.

Walker, T. 2006. Slave or Soldiers? African Conscripts in Portuguese India, 1857–1860. In *Slavery and South Asian History*, ed. I. Chatterjee and R. Eaton. Bloomington: Indiana University Press.

Wilberforce-Bell, H. 1916. *A History of Kathiawar from the Earliest Times*. London: Heinemann.

Williams, E. 1944. *Capitalism and Slavery*. Chapel Hill: The University of North Carolina.

Willis, C. 2003. David Livingstone, Africa and the Portuguese. Occasional Paper Series 26, Department of Hispanic, Portuguese and Latin American Studies, University of Bristol.

Wink, A. 1990. Al Hind: *The Making of the Indo-Islamic World*. Delhi: Oxford University Press.

Worden, N. 2007. Revolt in Cape Colony Slave Society. In *Resisting Bondage in Indian Ocean Africa and Asia*, ed. E. Alpers, G. Campbell, and M. Salman. London and New York: Routledge.

Index

About the Author

Shihan de Silva Jayasuriya is a Senior Fellow at the Institute of Commonwealth Studies, University of London. She is a Fellow of the Royal Asiatic Society (Great Britain and Ireland). She is also associated with King's College, University of London. She has a PhD in Linguistics from the University of Westminster and two degrees from the University of London: an MSc in Finance and a BSc Honours in Economics.

Dr. de Silva Jayasuriya has published over eighty articles in peer-reviewed journals worldwide. She is also the author of four books: *Tagus to Taprobane* (Tisara Prakasakayo, Colombo, 2001); *An Anthology of Indo-Portuguese Verse* (Edwin Mellen Press, Wales, 2001); *Indo-Portuguese of Ceylon* (Athena Publications, London, 2001); and *Portuguese in the East: Cultural History of a Maritime Trading Empire* (I. B. Tauris, London, 2008). She co-edited (with Professor Richard Pankhurst) *The African Diaspora in the Indian Ocean* (Africa World Press, New Jersey, 2003). She is the co-founder of TADIA (The African Diaspora in Asia), a program associated with the UNESCO Slave Route Project.